100 Things To Know Before You Go

Real Life Stories of an Exchange Student in America

Scott P. Staber and Dominique Kirste
An American Dad and his German Exchange Daughter

PublishAmerica
Baltimore

First printing

Hardcover 978-1-4560-7236-0
Softcover 978-1-4560-7237-7
PUBLISHED BY PUBLISHAMERICA, LLLP
www.publishamerica.com
Baltimore

Printed in the United States of America

Dedication:

This book is dedicated to exchange students throughout the world and to the families and volunteers around America who make cultural exchange a possibility.

Dedication:

This book is dedicated to exchange students throughout the world and to the families and volunteers around America who make cultural exchange a possibility.

Acknowledgements:

This book would not have been possible without the guidance and support of friends and family in America and Germany. Special thanks are given to Michelle Staber, Alec Staber, Abi Staber, Rainer Kirste, Ute Kirste and Madeleine Kirste for boundless support and encouragement. We are grateful for the assistance in ideas and editing by Lexyann Staber, Jeffrey Heydanek and Ann Ruhman.

Foreword:

This book was written to provide past, present and future exchange students with information about life in America in a fun and personal format. Our research found that most exchange books are straight forward how-to books that, although insightful, are not necessarily easy to read. It was our intent to provide the reader with simple English language stories about 100 uniquely American topics. Each subject is discussed in storybook format as written by both a host parent and an exchange student. Mixed in with these stories you will find interesting trivia, facts and tips about each subject. Finally, we have added trivia about each state in America; learning these may give you a start of you first history exam. Although the book has a beginning and an ending, it can easily be read from topic to topic, in an order that the reader finds more interesting. We hope this book will bring back wonderful memories for past students and help future students discover their new upcoming life in America.

- Scott Staber and Dominique Kirste

Chapter 1—Coming and Going

What to know before you leave home and what to know before you return to your country. This chapter will provide you with necessary information about your trip and things that will help you never to forget the biggest adventure of your life.

Chapter 2—Around the House

Everything you want to know about your temporary American home, family and community. This chapter will guide you through the everyday life that you will be living for the next five to ten months.

Chapter 3—School Stuff

You heard American schools were completely different? You heard correctly, but don't worry, this chapter will give you the basics needed to get by and soon you will be just another typical American student.

Chapter 4—Holidays and Free Time

It's not all hard work at school and home. During your stay you are going to experience many holidays and you will have plenty of free time to enjoy your new American lifestyle. Take advantage of this time and experience America first hand.

CHAPTER 1
COMING AND GOING

HOST PARENT

1 - HOST FAMILY CONTACT

It was really exciting to hear from our exchange student within several days after we made our choice. Remember that being a host family is similar to being an exchange student—we get to learn about your culture and we get to be a part of your life. Getting to know each other a little bit before you arrive is helpful in preparing for your stay. Host families can tell you want will be needed and what might not be so important to pack. We exchanged e-mails for several months prior to her arrival date. By the time our exchange student was with us, we felt that we knew just enough to make her comfortable and had some school and housing items resolved. During the time our exchange student was in America we were in contact with her family, which was not only fun but comforting for everybody. These original contacts are just the beginning of a lifelong communication you may have with your host family.

DID YOU KNOW?
In 2010, there were approximately 294 billion e-mails sent every day, which are over 2.8 million e-mails per second. Unfortunately over 90% of them are spam and viruses. (1)

AMERICAN SLANG
I was "clueless" about my host family until we finally made contact.
(This means you have no idea or did/do not know anything about it.)

STATE of the UNION
Florida Nickname - Sunshine State

EXCHANGE STUDENT

1 - HOST FAMILY CONTACT

As soon as you are notified who your host family is, you should contact them by sending an e-mail, a letter, or if you are brave enough, you may even give them a call. I decided to send an e-mail and formally introduce myself and let my host family know how excited I was that they chose me. I also had many questions about my stay and this was a great way to find out information about my future home, family, school and community. I actually received an e-mail back the next day from my host sister and it was soon followed by more e-mails from my host parents and my host brother. This e-mail communication, prior to my trip, was very informative and helpful. I learned much about my host family, school, classes, and planned activities before I even left my own country. It was also nice to become acquainted before my arrival because when I finally arrived it already seemed like we knew each other.

TIPS...

- Write your new host family an e-mail as soon as you get their address. They will be just as excited about hearing from you as you are.
- Ask questions about your new family, home and community.
- Ask them if there is anything special or necessary that you should bring.
- Don't forget to thank them for picking you.

HOST PARENT

2 - PASSPORT and VISA

This book was intended to be fun and certainly not boring, but what could we do? Passports and visas are required and there is hardly anything exciting about the process. Without them, your exchange trip is not going to happen. A passport is a document issued by your country that certifies your identity and nationality. The passport will contain a photo of you, your date of birth, location of birth and your sex. Make sure you get your passport in plenty of time before your trip. In some countries it may be a lengthy process from the time of your application to the receipt of your passport. A visa is a document or a stamp issued by the United States providing approval for entrance into the country for a specific reason. You will be receiving a student visa that will be dated for the time period of your exchange trip. Your exchange program will provide the specifics, but make sure you follow directions explicitly and on time or your trip may not get off the ground.

DID YOU KNOW?

Since the terrorist attack on the World Trade Center on September 11, 2001, travel to and from the United States has become much more difficult. Make sure all your documents are in order and always keep them is a secure place. We recommend you keep a copy in your luggage just in case your originals gets lost.

AMERICAN SLANG

Make sure you carry your "I.D." whenever you travel in America. (Saying the letters I and D is often used instead of using the word identification.)

EXCHANGE STUDENT

2 - PASSPORT and VISA

Unless you already live in a big city that has an American Consulate then you will soon be on the first trip of your exchange experience. Upon receipt of your passport and the proper forms provided to you by your exchange company (written in English so you can get some early practice) you will be required to travel to the consulate and apply for your student visa. The Consulate has many strict rules regarding entrance to the building and proper completion of required documents. It is important that you prepare properly and ensure that you have everything you need when you go to the Consulate. All paperwork must be present and in order or you may leave without accomplishing your requirements. Prepare to spend several hours, but depending on the day you may finish in as little as thirty minutes. If all goes as planned, you will leave the American Consulate without your passport but within several days it will arrive at your house with your student visa.

FACTS...

- You may not be allowed to enter the Consulate with your parents.
- You will probably be required to go through several security checks and have your fingerprints will be taken.
- You will most likely not be allowed to take in your cell phone and paperwork may be required to be carried in a clear folder.

STATE of the UNION

Maine State Capital - Augusta

HOST PARENT

3 - RESEARCH

Although you cannot pick exactly where you will live in America, you will know where you are heading prior to your departure. You will have plenty of time to research your upcoming American experience. As a host parent, I was also interested in learning about the town, country and culture of our exchange student. Research that we conducted prior to the arrival of our student gave us much to talk about during the first few days of the exchange year. This research also allowed us to prepare for some things our student may not be used to and it gave us ideas for discussions to make it easier for her to adjust to our family and to her new life in America. Purchasing this book may be the first step in your research, but make sure it is not your last. Use the information you have found throughout this book to discover more about America, including your town, school, or anything that you want to experience during your stay.

DID YOU KNOW?

Our own research while writing this book found that not all students have a perfect year in America and some will actually have a bad experience. Do your best and prepare before you go. You will significantly increase your chances to have a perfect year in the United States.

AMERICAN SLANG

The research I conducted made it easy to "break the ice" with my host family. (This is to start something or getting to know somebody.)

STATE of the UNION

Alabama Nickname - Cotton State

EXCHANGE STUDENT

3 - RESEARCH

The first thing I did when I received my host family's e-mail was to use the Internet to research my future American hometown and my high school on the Internet. I checked out several homepages and found lots of information and many photographs of my new school and town. If that does not get you excited then your exchange organization will. Most exchange companies will require you to attend some type of orientation or prep camp before you go, where you will learn things about typical American life and school. Make sure that you go because they have already researched things, like how to open your American school locker. Believe me; it's not as easy as it looks! In addition to this, I read some books written by former exchange students to see what their experiences were like and to help prepare for my trip. Finally, the best research advice in my opinion: Watch some of the famous American High School movies! They are often a bit exaggerated but basically they show what life is like in America! My favorite is *High School Musical* and my host dad's favorite is *The Breakfast Club*. A couple other fun ones to watch are *Clueless*, *Mean Girls*, *Bring it On* and *Napoleon Dynamite*.

TIPS...

- Conduct an internet search about your American state and city on *Wikipedia* or other information web sites.
- Search for city and state web sites that will provide you with much information about your new home.
- Search the address of your American home on *Google Earth* and see exactly what it looks like from the sky.
- Virtually all American school districts have web sites where you can find just about anything you might want to know.

HOST PARENT

4 - PACKING

I'm sure your exchange company will tell you how to pack and what you will need, but it is the responsibility of your host family to have a place for you to unpack your stuff. I've seen some students living out of their suitcases, others sharing storage space with siblings and still others with more space than they could possibly need. Whatever ends up being your style and your situation, there is one packing rule that will never change—you will be packing more for your trip home than you do for your trip to America. Think about it and you will see what I mean: Christmas presents, birthday presents, new clothes, scrapbooks, school yearbooks, souvenirs, projects and many more items too numerous to put on this page. If you have room you may want to pack an extra bag that can fold up inside of your luggage or you may want to budget some money to mail some of your extra stuff home just before you leave. Whatever is your situation, you may find packing the most difficult challenge of your exchange experience.

DID YOU KNOW?
American appliances and electronics run on 110 volts and have unique shaped plugs. American plugs have two flat prongs. Don't forget to bring a converter if you want to use electronics you brought from home.

AMERICAN SLANG
I was in a real "pickle" deciding how many pairs of shoes to pack. (When you have a tough time deciding or are confused about something.)

STATE of the UNION
Nevada State Capital - Carson City

EXCHANGE STUDENT

4 - PACKING

"Don't forget this, don't forget that! Did you put this in your pile?" I was tired of my mom telling me what to pack and was it really necessary for me to pack several weeks in advance? As so often is the case, my mom was right and I quickly became thankful that she was so persistent. She put several boxes in my bedroom and we would put items in them as we thought of them. I also made a list which was very helpful when I was not able to box it yet or if I still needed to find or purchase the item. The day before I left I had to transfer everything to my suitcases and conduct my final purging. In other words, determining what I really needed to take or wanted to take and leaving items that were not so important. When I unpacked in America it turned out that I didn't miss a thing, so make your lists, start packing early and good luck trying to fit a year's worth of items into just one or two bags.

TIPS...

- Pack dress shoes and dress pants for special events you will be attending.
- Find out your new "school colors" and bring some matching clothes.
- Roll clothing to get more in your suitcase.
- Consider packing another bag for all the extra stuff you will be taking home.
- Always pack your medications, jewelry and other valuables in your carry-on bag so they do not get lost or stolen.
- Before you leave for the U.S., lay out everything you want to bring and then leave half of it home because you probably won't need it all.

HOST PARENT

5 - COMMUNICATION

Our own research in preparing for our exchange student kept stressing how important it is to be patient and speak slowly. We were also told that after several days the language change would just "turn on" and that communication would no longer be a concern. That is exactly what happened. After several days we were having easy conversations with our new family member. It is so important to talk in order to learn. The more you talk the easier the language will become. We played word games with our exchange daughter. *"Apples to Apples"* is a fun game that greatly improved her vocabulary. (This will be your hardest obstacle...do you know what obstacle means?) When you don't understand a word or a sentence, make sure you ask so you can pack in as much learning as possible. If you miss an opportunity to find out what a word means, don't worry, you will know enough other words in the conversation to understand what is being discussed.

DID YOU KNOW?

America is so big that there are many accents within the country. You will find strong language differences between people from the South, the Midwest, the Northeast, Texas and California. Ya'll see what we mean when you stay for a while.

AMERICAN SLANG

My host sister sure likes to "yak" a lot. (To yak is to talk.)

EXCHANGE STUDENT

5 - COMMUNICATION

I will be honest with you now, the first day or two is going to be tough. I'm not afraid to admit that changing languages for the first time was difficult, but it did not last long. When I arrived in America and I met my host family, it seemed like I forgot everything I had learned in English class. Everybody, especially my host sister, talked so fast that I could not understand a single word they were saying. For the first couple hours I felt like the family dog who can't understand anything except their own name. Just hang in there because you are about to learn English better than any of your classmates back in your home country (most of them anyways). It really is true that the best way to learn a language is to speak it all the time. You will learn so much that before long you will not remember what you learned at school and what you learned in America. Believe it or not, I was soon forgetting some of my German language and, yes, I was even dreaming in English...

TIPS...

Don't be afraid to:

- Ask your host family to "slow down" if they are talking faster than you can keep up.
- Ask what a word means when you don't understand, it is the only way to build your vocabulary.

STATE of THE UNION

Ohio Nickname - Buckeye State

HOST PARENT

6 - AIRPLANE RIDE

No matter where your trip begins, you are most likely going to be stuck on a long airplane ride. It is my opinion that your airplane trips to and from your home will be the most difficult days of your entire experience. Mixing the difficulties of long distance travel with your nervous emotions can make these trips very stressful. Remember that this exchange year is not only about learning and experiencing another culture, but it is also about learning and obtaining your independence. Your very first day away from home will immediately require you to find your way, ask questions, make decisions and follow directions, and all in a language you are just learning. Upon making it safely to your American destination and meeting your host family, you will have successfully jumped the first hurdle. Everything from this point on will be easy...until your trip back home. Once again, you will be fighting the roller coaster of emotions that comes with leaving a new family and going home to your family. Grab a pillow and a blanket, lean back in your chair and dream about how much your life has changed.

DID YOU KNOW?

According to the Summit Medical Group it takes 1 day of recovery for each time zone crossed when travelling east to west and 1.5 days of recovery for each time zone crossed when travelling west to east. (2)

AMERICAN SLANG

My exchange organization booked me on the "red eye" flight. (This is a plane that leaves late in evening and travels all night long.)

STATE of the UNION

Texas State Capital - Austin

EXCHANGE STUDENT

6 - AIRPLANE RIDE

You might not even be thinking about your plane ride right now, but you should. The trip to America and the trip home were both much more difficult than I expected. Leaving your family and your friends might sound like fun right now, but it was very difficult when the time actually came to go through the airport gate. If that isn't bad enough, it was almost as difficult leaving my family and friends in America when it was time to go home. Except for the long car rides to international airports, the actual plane rides were long but exciting. Crossing the Atlantic Ocean took a while, but my friends from Asia had much longer trips (and my trips were 16 hours from door to door). During the plane rides I had plenty to do to make the trips seem shorter. I listened to music on my MP3 player, I read my book, and I watched in-flight movies, but no matter how much I tried to sleep, I couldn't. I was just too excited. After I picked up my luggage and went through customs I finally made it to my destination. Both coming and going I was greeted by family and friends with posters that read "Wilkommen (welcome) Dominique".

TIPS...

- Grab a pillow and blanket as soon as you get on the plane.
- If you have a choice, pick a window seat so you can put your pillow against the window/wall.
- Drink plenty of liquids on your flight.
- Before traveling east go to bed earlier for several days before your flight and later for your westward flight.
- Don't forget to carry-on your MP3 player, your current book and several magazines.

HOST PARENT

7 - INTRODUCTION GIFTS

It was a special day when our exchange student arrived and had a fantastic ending when our exchange student gave us gifts. We had so much fun opening them and even more fun having some of our first conversations regarding her home, village, family and friends. It was the perfect beginning to a perfect year with our exchange student. Remember that one of the reasons your host family has opened their home and their hearts is to not only provide you with an opportunity, but to also learn about you and your culture. If you are going to bring gifts, you should consider bringing something that represents your life, your culture and your interests. You don't need to spend a lot of money, homemade gifts and little novelties are best. Remember, your host family is not expecting anything and you are not required to bring anything, but I have found that host families are special people and anything you bring as a "thank you" gift will be greatly appreciated. I will admit that it is a great kickoff to a fun year for you and your host family.

DID YOU KNOW?

The Statue of Liberty, which is a prominent symbol of the United States, was a gift from France in 1886 as a celebration of 100 years of independence and friendship with France. If you travel to New York City, make sure you visit this landmark. (3)

STATE of the UNION

Illinois Nickname - The Land of Lincoln

EXCHANGE STUDENT

7 - INTRODUCTION GIFTS

Think about it, your host family is taking you into their household and their life for one year. They have given you something you can't buy—a home and a family. They have volunteered to host you and are willing to make you part of their family and this you should not take for granted. Always remember that this is a change for them and during my time in America I found out how much of a commitment my host family actually made. For these reasons I am glad I made a decision to bring welcome gifts. You can bring anything you like, but during your pre-trip conversations you will likely find out something about your new family that may help you decide what you should bring. I brought candy to share, music (CDs) for my new siblings and several books about my hometown, but without a doubt, the favorite gift of my host family was the homemade photo scrapbook I made of my life and culture in Germany. It was a gift from the heart and those are always the best kind of gifts.

TIPS...

- Make a scrapbook or a photo album of your life at home.
- Bring sweets or snacks from your country.
- Bring music, art or books about your culture.
- Bring games or small trinkets popular in your country.

AMERICAN SLANG

I picked up a few "doo dads" for my exchange family.

(These are things or objects that are not specifically identified or known.)

HOST PARENT

8 - ARRIVAL and FIRST DAY

You may think that you are the only excited and nervous person, but I can assure you that your new host family has many of the same feelings. It is very possible that your host family has hosted other students, but it is just as possible to get a rookie family like ours. We did not know what to expect any more than our exchange student did, and therefore our first meeting and our first day was a bit awkward. That only lasted for a short time. After our student adjusted to the time change, to the new surroundings and became comfortable conversing in English, then it was as if she was always part of the family. This first day and the first week after your arrival may be a bit difficult, but from what I've seen, you will be talking, laughing, learning and becoming a short term American kid very quickly. So don't worry too much because, before you know it, you'll be excited and nervous about going back home.

DID YOU KNOW?

Jetlag is a term used to describe a temporary disruption of bodily rhythms caused by high speed travel across several time zones. (4)

AMERICAN SLANG

I finally get to spend some real "face time" with my host family. (This is actual time you spend together and not time over the phone or chatting on the computer.)

STATE of the UNION

Kansas State Capital - Topeka

EXCHANGE STUDENT

8 - ARRIVAL and FIRST DAY

Almost there...according to the small white plane showing on the airplane TV (television) screens. It was soon time to meet the family I would be living with for the next year. It is normal at this time to feel really excited, happy and very nervous. It took about an hour to disembark, retrieve my luggage and go through customs. It was time; I walked through the doors to find a family waiting with a sign that read "Herzlich Willkommen Dominique!" I met my new family, snapped our first photo and then we were off. Once we were in the car heading to my new home it seemed like I forgot everything I learned in English class. My nerves combined with jetlag and the excessive speed at which my new host sister spoke made my first few hours very difficult. I moved into my new room, met my new pets, walked around the new neighborhood, called my parents, exchanged presents and went directly to bed. I was here, I was comfortable, I was happy and I was exhausted. The first day was long, but it was a great beginning to a great year.

TIPS...

- It is normal to be nervous.
- It is going to be one of the longest days of your life.
- It will take you several days until you understand everything that is being said.
- Have trust in what you have learned in English class and jump right in.
- Being scared is normal, but you will soon feel like a movie star since everybody is going to want to meet you.

HOST PARENT

9 - TIME ZONES

Why do we need to talk about time zones? Everybody knows about time zones, but in America we have six of them (not counting territories). If you are from Russia then I guess this is about half of what you are used to, but you may, never-the-less, want to know about them. Starting from the east coast of the United States we have the Eastern Time Zone, the Central Time Zone, the Mountain Time Zone, the Pacific Time zone, the Alaskan time zone and the Hawaiian time zone. You have about a 50% chance of living in a State within the Eastern Time Zone since approximately half of the U.S. population resides in this time zone. Don't fret because within this time zone you can find some of the most historic areas, some beautiful winter wonderlands and, of course, our most popular tropical paradise—Florida. Get on the Internet and discover all the beautiful States in America. No matter which time zone you will live, there will be beautiful sights and fun activities.

DID YOU KNOW?

In America ST stands for "Standard Time" while in Europe and some other areas ST stands for "Summer Time" which is the equivalent of the American "Daylight Savings Time" or DST.

AMERICAN SLANG

After traveling all day you are going to be ready to "hit the sack". (It's time to go to bed and get some sleep.)

STATE of the UNION

Rhode Island Nickname - Ocean State

EXCHANGE STUDENT

9 - TIME ZONES

Between Europe and America there is a difference of between six and ten hours and from Asia there is a difference of between eight and twelve hours. Keeping this in mind, the day you leave for America could be the longest day of your life (or at least it will feel like it). You may even be arriving from a location at the same time you left only to lose all that time when you go home. Confused? I was too. All I know is that when I left from Germany in the morning, I arrived in America in the mid afternoon and still had eight hours before bed time...I was completely exhausted. If you get the opportunity to travel within the United States, whether by car or plane, it is possible you will be crossing time zones. What looks like a short distance on a map may actually be a long way in reality. You will need to always be aware of your time zone when talking to friends and family at home because it may be necessary for you to call them at limited times when everybody is available and more importantly...awake.

FACTS...

- In America we say "Spring Forward and Fall Back" in order to not forget which way to move our clocks during time changes.
- Some U.S. States do not observe Daylight Savings Time.
- America uses the 12 hour clock using A.M. and P.M. while only the U.S. Military uses the 24 hour clock.

HOST PARENT

10 - HOME PHOTOS

Soldiers usually carry one thing from home with them while in battle—a photograph. Whether a photo of a girlfriend, mother or a family member, nothing can get you back home quicker than a photograph. Life is nothing more than experiences and memories that are stored in your brain and often times on a small piece of photographic paper. There will no doubt be times when you will miss your family and your friends during your time away from home, so what better way to cheer up your day than looking at several of your favorite photographs from home. Our exchange daughter brought a handful of photos to hang up, several small photo albums and a hand-made photo calendar given to her by her best friends. Before you know it you will be hanging photos of your new friends and your host family in your own bedroom so you can always be close to those memories you created in America.

DID YOU KNOW?

The word photography is Greek and when defined, it essentially means to draw with light (phots = light and graphein = drawing). Joseph Nicephore Niepce is credited with the very first photograph in 1827. (5)

AMERICAN SLANG

Everybody say "cheese"! (This is what you say to get everybody in the photograph to smile right before you take a picture.)

STATE of the UNION

Hawaii State Capital - Honolulu

EXCHANGE STUDENT

10 - HOME PHOTOS

The first thing you should pack for your extended trip away from home is photographs. You are not going to see your family and friends for a year and photographs are a great way of seeing them every day. My host family put up a bulletin board, and gave me several frames to use for displaying my photos. This kept me close to my family while at the same time it decorated my room with some of my favorite things. My host family and friends were also very interested in my life at home and sharing my favorite friends, places, and interests in the way of photographs made it easy and fun. While you are away make sure that your family e-mails you more photos so you can actually see what is happening back home. Smile and say "cheese" as they say in America.

TIPS...

- Digital photography provides you with the ability to take as many pictures as you want. Take a lot so you remember your entire year and so you can share your memories at home.
- Organize your photos with dates and place names as soon as possible, otherwise 10 months of photos can be a lot to organize at home.
- Remember to charge your battery and have enough room on your memory card before you leave on a trip or activity.
- Making a copy of your digital photos to leave with your host family makes a great going-away present.

HOST PARENT

11 - SCHOOL NEEDS

No matter what country you are from, I am sure that your American school is going to be different in many ways. I have been told by many students that it is almost exactly like what you see in your favorite American movies. As soon as you arrive you will probably have to pick your classes and, in most cases, you are going to have many more choices than you do now. This usually takes place before the school year begins at which time you will also have your school photo taken and your student ID made. You will buy photo packages and give photos to your friends and send some home to your family. If you are going to play a sport, you may need to bring your equipment or plan on purchasing it while you are here (such as a tennis racquet or shin guards). Don't forget to order your yearbook, which is a published photo album of your school year, and you can even buy a class ring with engravings that represent your school and your activities or interests. Depending on your schedule you may need to bring your really good calculator and don't forget...and don't forget...and well, I forgot.

DID YOU KNOW?
You can bring your lunch to school and it is called a "packed lunch" or a "cold lunch" while if you buy your lunch at school it is typically called a "hot lunch". This is the case even if the purchased lunch is not actually hot.

AMERICAN SLANG
You may need to bring some of your "thingamabobs" to school. (These are your "things" or your "stuff".)

STATE of the UNION
Arizona Nickname - Grand Canyon State

EXCHANGE STUDENT

11 - SCHOOL NEEDS

My German school required me to take English, French, math, science and social studies while in America so it would not be necessary for me to repeat the eleventh grade when I returned home. That was a lot of required classes considering that I could only pick six classes in total at my American School. Fortunately, American schools have many choices of classes that we don't have the opportunity to take in my school at home. Some of my exchange student friends were able to take anything they wanted depending on what country (or school) they were coming from. Some students took nothing other than "fun" classes and hopefully you will be as lucky as they were. If you get the opportunity to pick your classes before you leave for America, you may be able to find out what things you may need as we have listed in the "tips" section. Do not hesitate to take what they call AP (Advanced Placement) classes if at all possible. You may find that your school at home is more challenging than your American school and these AP classes are for advanced students preparing for college and are possibly similar to your level of study.

TIPS...

- **All Classes -** Pencils, pens and notebooks/paper (not supplied)
- **Dance** - leotards and dance shoes
- **Photography** - 35mm camera
- **Math** - calculator
- **Sports** - gym shoes, shorts, protective gear (e.g., shin guards)

HOST PARENT

12 - CURRENCY

It is said that "money is a necessary evil" since without it survival is just about impossible. Your exchange trip is most likely your first time to be so far away from home without your family. It is probably the first time you will manage your own finances. While my exchange daughter will explain the types of coin and currency that are in America, there are a few other money related items you should keep in mind. First, don't forget to check out the exchange rate you will receive for currency from your home country. It is very unlikely that you will receive an equal trade for your money. In many cases you may actually do better if your currency is stronger than the U.S. dollar. Second, taxes are likely different than in your home country. Although all U.S. States are different, most have some type of sales tax which is normally not identified on the price tag. When you arrive find out what is taxed and how much the tax is and this will assist you in figuring out what you will really be paying on items that you purchase. You will probably find some great deals, but don't forget to manage your money properly since there are many things you will want to do during your stay.

DID YOU KNOW?

For 10 years starting in 1999, the United States Mint 50 State Quarters Program released a quarter designed for each of the 50 states. Which state first? The states were honored in age order—oldest first—according to when they ratified the Constitution or joined the Union.

STATE of the UNION

Oklahoma State Capital - Oklahoma City

EXCHANGE STUDENT

12 - CURRENCY

American coins and currency are easy, but it does take some getting used to. Coins are also given names and everybody uses the names in conversation; a penny is 1 cent, a nickel is 5 cents, a dime is 10 cents and a quarter is 25 cents. One dollar coins are now available, but are rarely used and they are very unpopular since one dollar paper bills have been used for years. Other common paper money includes the five dollar bill, ten dollar bill, twenty dollar bill, fifty dollar bill and the one hundred dollar bill. You should make sure that you leave your country with some American money in case you get stuck at an airport and need food or a place to sleep. Don't ever carry too much money since there are cash machines everywhere and since most places accept credit cards. A credit card is important and you should seriously consider using one to obtain money whenever needed. You can also make arrangements in your home country for bills to be delivered to your home.

FACTS...

- A nickel is the only U.S. coin named after its metal content.
- The word nickel dates back to 1750 Germany and means rascal, so kupfernickel means false copper. In other words, nickel looks like copper which is more valuable than nickel. (6)

TIPS...

- It can be difficult trying to change currencies in the United States so you should not bring large amounts of money in your home currency to America.

AMERICAN SLANG

You can buy the best cookies at our school for just one "buck". (One buck equals one dollar.)

HOST PARENT

13 - METRICS

Incredibly, we still use an old system of measurement known simply as U.S. customary units. The rest of the world uses the metric system as do much of the American scientific, engineering and medical professions. As the world continues to get smaller through advances in technology and transportation, it is likely that the U.S. will eventually lose these archaic (old) units. You will probably know less about our system of measurement than your new American family and friends know about the metric system. Although this may be a bit of an inconvenience, you will have no problem adjusting, although your host family may need to answer questions like why they have a gallon of milk and a two liter bottle of Coke. The biggest problem comes when you attempt to cook from metric memorized recipes while having to utilize the American measuring devices...but that is all part of the fun.

DID YOU KNOW?

The United States is lost somewhere between the English (Imperial or Standard) System and the Metric System. You will observe temperature and speeds listed in the old system while some things like sporting events and beverages may be listed in the metric system.

AMERICAN SLANG

There was a lot of "hype" in the 1970's about America changing to the metric system. (Hype can be defined as excitement and exaggeration.)

STATE of the UNION

West Virginia Nickname - Mountain State

EXCHANGE STUDENT

13 - METRICS

Are you kidding me? I weigh 125 according to the scale. Can I really survive in this 90 degree heat? Fortunately my weight was measured in pounds and the temperature was measured in Fahrenheit, which are approximately 57 Kilos and 32 degrees Celsius. You will be surprised how often you refer to various units of measurements on a daily basis. Besides your body weight or the temperature you will need to convert speed (car speed is measured in miles per hour), cooking measurements and length. Did you know there are 12 inches to a foot and 3 feet to a yard and 1,760 yards to a mile? And what is a mile anyway? Most importantly, if you like to shop like I do, you will need to carry a handy size converter so you can find that perfect pair of jeans you may have been looking forward to buying during your stay in America. Maybe you can take this book to the store with you...

CONVERSIONS...

Shoe Size Conversions:

Women		*Men*	
US	Euro	US	Euro
6	36/37	8	41
8	39	9	43
10	41/42	10.5	44
12	44	11.5	45/46

Clothing Size Conversions:

Women		*Men*	
US	Euro	US	Euro
6	36	30	40
8	38	32	42
10	40	34	44
12	42	36	46

HOST PARENT

14 - CULTURE SHOCK

There is much more to culture shock than you realize so my host daughter and I are going to split this topic. I'll take the first two phases and she will take the second two phases. The first phase is fun and is appropriately called the "honeymoon" phase. Honeymoons are wonderful vacations with a new partner and when you first arrive that is how it will feel. Everything is new and you will be happy and excited to learn all about your new culture, family and friends. At first you will only see the things that in your opinion are good and possibly better than in your own country. The second phase you will go through is called "negotiation" and this is the time that you will begin to compare your new country against your home country. You will notice differences, observe attitudes, identify negative aspects and you will begin to wish you were back in your own country where things are familiar and comfortable. But don't worry, you will adjust...

DID YOU KNOW?

The word culture has many different definitions. In 1952 Alfred Kroeber and Clyde Klockhom published a book that contains 164 different definitions of culture titled *"Culture: A Critical Review of Concepts and Definitions".* (7)

AMERICAN SLANG

I think these culture shock phases are completely "twisted". (If you are twisted you are acting crazy or strange.)

STATE of the UNION

Minnesota State Capital - St. Paul

EXCHANGE STUDENT

14 - CULTURE SHOCK

Thanks for the great segue since "adjustment" is the third phase that I went through during my own culture shock experience. During this phase (and by the way this was by far the longest phase) I got used to my everyday life in America and I developed routines just as I did in my home country. I went to school, hung out with friends, participated in activities, had dinner, did homework, went to bed, etc. etc. My routine in America became as normal to me as my routine back home even though it was completely different. Finally, the biggest surprise to me was phase four; "reverse culture shock". Who would have guessed that going home would be so hard? Leaving your exchange life behind to change cultures and routines again is very difficult and may even be the toughest part of your whole experience. Was it worth it? No question about it, I would not think twice about going through these phases again for the chance to see more, learn more and further extend my family and friends.

TIPS...

- Try not to compare your usual life with the life you are living in America. Accept the differences as fun and temporary to help ease your concerns.
- If you begin thinking about how much better it is at home then it is probably time to find your friends and go do something.
- Time will take care of everything. After a month or so you will feel as good as you do at home.

HOST PARENT

15 - CLIMATE

Since you do not typically have a choice where you are going, it is possible that you could be in any kind of climate. Unfortunately for our exchange daughter, we had a very similar climate to her real home in Germany. But America has many different climates so there is a very good possibility that you will be living in a completely different climate. Maybe you will live in the deserts of the southwest or possibly in the often rainy areas of the northwest. The Midwest of America covers a wide area and receives all types of weather including heavy winter snowfall and hot summer days. We recently met a family in Florida who also had a German exchange student and who was lucky enough to be on a Florida beach for the entire year (just don't tell my exchange daughter who had to deal with several feet of snow). Just remember, no matter where you live, it is the people you meet and the friends you make that are more important than the amount of sunshine or snowfall.

DID YOU KNOW?

North America is the only continent that has every type of climate and the United States has most of them, from the tropics of Florida to the cold tundra of northern Alaska. You may need to pack a swimsuit, a winter jacket or both.

AMERICAN SLANG

We had a "crummy" weekend since it rained Friday, Saturday and Sunday. (Crummy is a good way of saying something is bad.)

STATE of the UNION

New York Nickname - Empire State

EXCHANGE STUDENT

15 - CLIMATE

I did not care what kind of climate I was going to live in during my exchange year as long as I was going to live in America. All I knew about the American climate before I left was that it could get really cold in the north and really hot in the south. In one of the first e-mails, my host family told me to bring warm clothes for the winter because Michigan can get really cold. I looked up Michigan and realized it is right on the border to Canada and so that must mean cold. When I was told we would be vacationing in Florida I found out that it reached all the way into the warm Caribbean Ocean. During spring break we traveled to Arizona where I was able to experience hot desert weather. I wasn't disappointed about living in Michigan because I love snow, although it wasn't easy to find people who enjoyed it as much as I did. I was surprised to find that Michigan could get so hot in the summer and that Arizona could get so cold in the winter. When it comes to climate in America you will find it all and very possibly you will experience it all. Bring clothes for all seasons and don't let the weather stop you from experiencing everything you can in America.

FACTS...

- Climate change is debated in America as much as anywhere else in the World.
- American politics do not always reflect the opinions of the American citizens and most Americans are concerned about climate change.
- Although slow to change, American cars are getting smaller and emission standards are becoming stricter.

HOST PARENT

16 - MORE FOR YOUR BUDGET

Our experience has proven that your exchange organization will not know every single expense of your year in America. Also, we admit that we do not know them all either since everybody's experiences and interests are different. We do know one important fact: you will likely need a little more money than you planned. Sure, public school is free in America, but many of the "extra" things are not, as you will find on the next page. How about your home life in America? You may need to budget for travel costs for a family vacation or at the very least you will want to bring home souvenirs from your trip. Most exchange organizations have one or two scheduled trips and various group activities which will cost you extra. Many American kids go to the cinema and who can watch a movie without a bucket of popcorn and a soda pop? Shopping is a favorite activity of not only American kids, but especially exchange students looking to find some great deals. How about Christmas presents for two families and birthday presents for all your new friends? Finally, let's not forget about mailing stuff home which can be a pretty expensive thing to do. How about those school expenses?

DID YOU KNOW?

Did you know that one of the most difficult things to do during your year in America is budget your money wisely and develop a strategy with your parents for accessing money and paying for the many activities and needs?

AMERICAN SLANG

If you budget for all these extra things you will be "sitting pretty". (You will be doing well if you are sitting pretty.)

STATE of the UNION

Connecticut State Capital - Hartford

EXCHANGE STUDENT

16 - MORE FOR YOUR BUDGET

Yes, there are expenses in your American school that you need to consider for your budget when you are planning your trip. You may not experience all of these expenses because many of these things are not required, but most exchange students want to participate in a lot of these events and take home keepsakes from their exchange experience. All these things are common in American schools across the country, but there are probably a few at your American school I don't even know about. At the beginning of the school year you will have your pictures taken and photo packages are available for you to send copies to your family and hand out to your friends. Soon after school begins you will have to order your yearbook which is something you don't want to pass up. If you want to participate in after school activities you might also have to pay some extra fees for those. Class rings are very expensive and school dances can add up because you need to buy tickets, a dress or suit and maybe new shoes. There will also be a school store where you can buy cool clothes with your school name and mascot. There are also all the things that go along with end-of year parties and graduation (if you are allowed to participate). OK, I didn't mean to scare you, but rather prepare you for some costs you might not have thought about.

TIPS...

Some typical costs you may expect during your year:
Yearbook ($50.00), Class Ring ($300.00-$700.00), Pay-to-Play Sports ($75.00-$200.00 per sport), Dances ($25.00-$50.00), School Photos ($30.00-$75.00), Senior Cap & Gown ($50.00-$75.00), All Night Party ($50.00-$100.00), In-School Lunch ($3.00-$6.00 per day), Movie Ticket ($8.00 average).

HOST PARENT

17 - AMERICAN HISTORY

Almost everybody has heard the phrase that "America is the melting pot of the world" and maybe you have too. If you do not believe that it is true, you soon will. Most exchange students are required to take a class in American history and in that class you will discover that America has been built by immigrants from all over the world. Beginning with many European immigrants progressing through Africa, Asia and the other Americas (Central and South), the country grew. It truly is the most diverse nation in the world and the American people are very acceptable to all ethnicities, religions and cultures. After you have been here a while you will find that it is difficult putting clear definition on an "American". When you leave you will be surprised that you have American friends of many cultures. (I bet you thought America was just one culture didn't you?) This history keeps on writing itself over and over again and America continues to grow with immigrants from all over the world. Who knows, maybe you will be like my Grandfather and move to America. Everybody is welcome.

DID YOU KNOW?

Over 12 million immigrants entered the United States (1892-1954) through Ellis Island, New York. Although there were many other ports to enter into the U.S., Ellis Island became known as the Gateway to America and is now a national monument with the Statue of Liberty. (8)

AMERICAN SLANG

Those poor people must have felt pretty "grubby" after all those days on a ship. (You are dirty, sweaty and not clean.)

EXCHANGE STUDENT

17 - AMERICAN HISTORY

In the United States you will meet people that have ancestors from all over the world. I could not believe how many people I met with German names and German traditions. I was very surprised when a girl from my American school told me that she has always called a wash cloth a "Waschlappen" just because her great grandparents (born in Germany) had always used that word. Did you know that many American's say "Gesundheit" as often as they say "God Bless You"? I didn't either. There are so many people of Irish decent that St. Patrick's Day is a very popular holiday and everybody seems to be Irish for a day (even if you're Chinese). There are no American names, instead Americans have German names, Irish names, Polish names, Japanese names and, well, I think you get the idea. America really is a "melting pot" and it will only take you a few weeks to discover this for yourself. Sure, Europe and Asia have a long rich history, but America has people so diverse in heritage and culture, it really is like the whole world has come to live in one place.

FACTS...

According to the 2010 U.S. Census: (9)

- Approximately 80% of Americans speak only English while 20% speak other languages (12% speak Spanish).
- Approximately 12% of America's population is foreign born of which 5% are currently U.S. citizens.
- There are approximately 35 million American households with children under 18 years old.
- Approximately 7.2% of Americans are between 15 & 19 years old...approximately 21 million.

STATE of the UNION

Missouri Nickname - Show Me State

HOST PARENT

18 - POSTAGE and PACKAGES

Let's be honest, no matter what your age, everybody loves to get stuff in the mail. You know your family will be sending you several packages throughout the year, but you will also be sending some things home. You are going to send home Christmas presents, birthday presents, letters and postcards, so you may want to budget a little money for this expense. Although there are several options for sending items overseas, we found the least expensive to be the U.S. Postal Service. Costs obviously depend on the size, weight and destination, but you need to plan on spending a minimum of $50.00 U.S. Dollars for a small, lightweight box of goodies. Letters and postcards are typically $1.00 for an airmail stamp and although the Internet has done a great job replacing real mail, it is still fun to get a hand written letter or a postcard from a trip you took. Our exchange daughter always smiled when she received any mail from home and she would often pin-up postcards or other items she received from friends and family.

DID YOU KNOW?

"The U.S. Postal Service delivers more mail to more addresses in a larger geographical area than any other post in the world. The USPS delivers to more than 149 million residences, businesses and post office boxes." (10)

AMERICAN SLANG

This letter will make it to Europe in one day "when pigs fly". (This means you think it will never happen.)

STATE of the UNION

New Mexico State Capital - Santa Fe

EXCHANGE STUDENT

18 - POSTAGE and PACKAGES

Just before I began my journey, I promised my friends and family that I would send letters and post cards to keep them up to date with all the cool things that I was expecting to experience. It was easy to forget and difficult to make time to write, but I always made time and I never forgot. Everybody at home truly appreciated the notes and cards I sent from America. And let's be honest, e-mails are so common now and so impersonal, everybody loves to get a hand written letter or a photograph describing a place they have only heard about, but have never seen. For my grandparents it was especially nice because they don't use the Internet nor do they have computers or e-mail addresses. Do you know what the best part of sending personal hand written messages by mail will be? That's correct, you will receive letters, post cards and even packages back. There is nothing better than enjoying your stay in America while at the same time receiving small memories of your home town by receiving photos, candy or gifts. Unfortunately you may even be sending packages to yourself. Yep, if you don't have room for all the stuff you've acquired in America, you'll be mailing them home just in time for you to open your own mail.

FACTS...

- You can find shipping cost information at www.usps.com, www.fedex.com/us, www.ups.com and www.dhl-usa.com.
- You can find a U.S. Post Office in almost every American city and you can find UPS stores in many suburban cities.
- Shipping supplies can be purchased at any office supply store and many large department stores. The UPS stores will even box your items for you if you don't want to do it yourself.

HOST PARENT

19 - HOMESICK

This may seem silly to you now, but I've seen several exchange students get pretty upset about being away from their home and their family. Even I have been homesick after being gone only a few days on a business trip. Homesickness is normal for exchange students and every student goes through it to some degree. A quick call home might just be enough to get you going again, but if you don't have that opportunity then get up and get moving. Do something with your host family or with your friends. I have found that whenever I am feeling down the best way for me to feel better is through activity. Our exchange daughter always stayed busy and if she got homesick she was an expert at covering it up. Don't forget to rely on your exchange student friends for support because they are in the same situation as you and they are experiencing the same feelings of anxiety and separation. Do not close yourself into your bedroom. Open up your concerns to the people in your exchange life and you will find many who are ready to help.

DID YOU KNOW?

Did you know many American kids attend college following high school? Most of these students will stay full-time at their university and many of them will experience homesickness for the first time. By then, you will already be an expert of homesickness.

AMERICAN SLANG

I was feeling really "blue" until I made a quick call home.

(If you are blue then you are sad.)

STATE of the UNION

Utah Nickname - Beehive State

EXCHANGE STUDENT

19 - HOMESICK

To be honest, I was afraid of getting homesick during my exchange year before I even turned in my application. I had never left my family for longer than one week and now I was planning on leaving for almost one year. It is a little frightening to know you are leaving your family and going so far away to a family you hardly know anything about. If you are anything like me, I am sure it is something you can't stop thinking about. In retrospect, I don't think I was ever homesick, but there were times when I really missed my family and friends. It is difficult to get homesick if you stay busy at school and at home. I kept a busy schedule and my host family always had many activities planned. It helped to talk to my family almost every weekend and to my friends every once in a while. Talking to your family at home can make the separation easier, but be careful how often you do it because it could backfire and only remind you of home more often. It's alright to be homesick, but not if it is so bad that it ruins your experience.

TIPS...

These tips are common sense, but they are not easy to do when you are feeling depressed:

- Be careful, exchange organizations do not recommend calling home because it may make your MORE homesick.
- Talk to a friend, your host family or a trusting adult.
- Do something. Don't sit around thinking about home.
- Look at photos you have brought from home that are on your wall or on your computer.
- Computer chats with friends and family at home.
- Write in your journal about your feelings or write an e-mail to your best friend back home.

HOST PARENT

20 - ACCENTS

It seems that most people think an accent is very weird or cool, but no matter what you think, accents are fun. Yes, no question about it—you are going to have an accent, but so will the other exchange students at your American high school. America is big so there are many accents within our country and every region seems to make fun of the other ones. If you visited long enough you could easily tell where a person is from in America, at least what region they are from. Here are some distinct examples: Midwest, New England, Southern or Western. Some States have distinct accents such as New York, Texas and California and, some people say, every State has their own accent. Our own predetermined opinion was that our exchange daughter was going to have a harsh German accent which turned out to be completely wrong. Apparently American movies exaggerate accents. My own Austrian Grandfather must have kept a heavy accent because he was proud of his heritage and wanted everybody to ask him about it.

DID YOU KNOW?

Did you know there is a significant difference between British English accents and American English accents? If you are not sure then go watch an American movie and find out which accent you may be learning at your school right now.

AMERICAN SLANG

Everybody thinks their own accent is the "cream of the crop". (The cream rises to the top and the top is the best.)

STATE of the UNION

Wisconsin State Capital - Madison

EXCHANGE STUDENT

20 - ACCENTS

Exchange students are always nervous about understanding English, but I think I was more nervous about my accent. As it turns out, my accent was not that bad and everybody loves listening to accents and trying to figure out where you are from. My host family liked (and still likes) to tease me about some of my English skills and the sounds I make trying to pronounce words correctly, but let your host family try your language and you'll admit that it is pretty funny. There are some German words (and sounds) that my host family and American friends could never seem to say correctly. My host family would help me a lot with my English language skills and they were very proud of my progress. After my year in American, my host family was sure that nobody could tell I was not their real American daughter (at least by listening to me speak since we look nothing alike). Finally, if you don't know it already, the American accent is much different than the accent from Great Britain and let's hope your English teacher from your real home isn't expecting you to speak like that because you are about to find out how much different American English really is.

FACTS...

- America is often described as a "melting pot" of cultures and you will not only find many different American accents but many European, Asian and African accents as well.
- Accents may be only part of your challenge while other difficulties may arise when some Americans speak so fast and others so slow.

HOST PARENT

21 - EXCHANGE ORGANIZATIONS

There are many exchange organizations to choose from and although many of them are very similar you should shop for the one that is right for you. Some are large and some are much smaller, while all have different costs for participating. Our experience with two completely different organizations were both positive and I believe most of these organizations have your best interest in mind. Most of these groups have been doing this for many years and have the experience and knowledge to make your experience go smoothly. The organization you choose in your home country will have information packages, forms, books and orientations. They will guide you through the process step by step until you reach America. Once you land you will be handed off to the American counter-part of your organization and the counseling and information will keep coming. So shop for your organization and choose one that fits your personality and budget. This organization is going to be a key in having a successful exchange year in the U.S.A.

DID YOU KNOW?

Did you know that almost all exchange organizations have three common important rules?

1. No Drinking (alcohol) or Drug Use
2. No Hitchhiking
3. No Driving (motorized vehicles)

Breaking any of these rules will send you straight home.

AMERICAN SLANG

Always listening to your exchange counselor is a good "rule of thumb".
(This is correct or it is the proper thing to do.)

STATE of the UNION

Louisiana Nickname - Pelican State

EXCHANGE STUDENT

21 - EXCHANGE ORGANIZATIONS

If you have searched "student exchange" on the Internet, you will have noticed that there are many companies who want to represent you. The best way to find out about these organizations is to talk to other people who have already been an exchange student. You can also research company information, talk to teachers at your school or even meet with families of past exchange students. Several of my friends recommended the organization that I used and after my first meeting I was sure I had made a good choice. All the people with the organization in my country and in America were very nice and able to answer all my questions and address all my concerns. I found that most people working for my exchange organization in my home country had been exchange students themselves and that most exchange program people in America have hosted students before. Most organizations arrange meetings and/or parties before you leave and after you arrive. Your exchange organization in America will also become like a family to you. You will no doubt make friends for life with one or several other students from your organization. It will be up to you to pick your exchange organization, but they will do a great job making your trip a success.

FACTS...

The U.S.A. issues J1 visas to exchange visitors participating in programs that promote cultural exchange such as those offered for high school exchange students. According to immigrationroad.com the 5 most J1 visas issued in 2008 went to people from: Russia (31,597), Germany (25,149), Brazil (21,125), China (20,578) and Great Britain/Northern Ireland (17,578). (11)

HOST PARENT

22 - SCRAPBOOKING

For all of you "male" students, scrapbooking might not be high on your list of things you want to do while staying in America, but just because most guys don't make scrapbooks does not mean that you can't give it a try. American host moms are great at scrapbooking and I'm sure you can talk your host mom into helping you. You might even be able to get your host mom to do it all if you trade her scrapbooking time for your time conducting some extra chores around the house. Even though I've never made one page in a scrapbook, I thoroughly enjoy looking at them. Scrapbooks are a great way to show the highlights of events over a long period of time. They never get boring to look at since each page is a snapshot of your best friends, your best times and your best memories.

DID YOU KNOW?

Scrapbooking is both creative and fun. People enjoy looking at scrapbooks as much as they enjoy making them. It is difficult to find a household in America that does not have a scrapbook to share family life.

AMERICAN SLANG

Making a scrapbook was a "piece of cake" for my host mom. (It was easy.)

STATE of the UNION

Alaska State Capital - Juneau

EXCHANGE STUDENT

22 - SCRAPBOOKING

Your exchange year will be one of the most exciting times of your life. Your experiences will be many, but it is hard to share everything with your family and friends back home during your stay. When you arrive home everybody is going to ask what you did. Will you remember everything from one month ago, or more likely, ten months ago? Don't forget to bring your camera! You should take pictures everywhere you go even if you are not going to make a scrapbook. But just remember, a year's worth of pictures is a lot and most likely they may end up in a big unorganized mess. In America, Scrapbooking is a very common hobby; it is a special technique of organizing your pictures in an album with theme related journals, stickers and decorations. You might get to see a couple good examples if your host mom is into scrapbooking and she may even be able to help you get started. Scrapbooking and writing a diary are two things you should do while you are in the United States because they will help you tell your story and most importantly, they will keep your memories forever.

FACTS...

- Approximately 1/3 of American households have one person who does scrapbooking. (12)
- Printed scrapbook paper was produced in Holland and Germany as early as the 1700's. (12)
- Both Queen Vitoria and Thomas Jefferson (the 3rd U.S. President) are said to have scrapbooks. (12)

HOST PARENT

23 - MYTHS

Well this is our one chance to convince you that some of the things you might hear about American people are just not true (or at least mostly not true). We are constantly told by our news media that foreigners think we are loud, obnoxious and arrogant people. True, Americans are honest and often say exactly how they feel, but most Americans are rarely intentionally rude. Like me, many Americans are uninhibited and enjoy social gatherings and lively conversations. So you think Americans like war? Nothing could be farther from the truth and, just like in your country, we have a political system that is often times not an exact representation of our people. What Americans do love is to help people who need help. No matter what you might see on television, I can promise you that there are thousands of Americans around the world trying to make a positive change. Whatever your opinions are now please put that on hold until you are here for a while, and let us prove that we have a whole lot in common.

DID YOU KNOW?

Did you know that if a myth is true then it is a fact? It is reported that 1/3 of Americans are obese and fast food, combined with lifestyle, is the likely source, but it should be noted that many countries are gaining weight too and some are even getting close to being as fat or fatter!! (13)

AMERICAN SLANG

These myths are just a "tip of the iceberg" when it comes to people's beliefs. (This often means it is only the beginning.)

STATE of the UNION

New Hampshire Nickname - Granite State

EXCHANGE STUDENT

23 - MYTHS

Exchange students are expected to have very good grades at school in their host country. *"No problem"*, was what former exchange students told me because *"Going to school in America is the easiest thing in the world."* But what you don't know is that America only has one kind of school and they have opportunities for all types of students. Good students take difficult and advanced classes while students that don't have as much ambition take an easier path. America is known to be the land of opportunity, but they also teach you that it is up to you to work hard and make your own opportunity. American schools have everything and it is up to you to decide on your own level of success. So is it easy? Yes, if you want it to be. How about all those wasteful Americans not caring one bit about our environment? Sure they drive big cars, but it is changing. There are even "smart" cars all over, but if you take one on the highway you are risking your life. Public transportation is getting better, everybody recycles, renewable energy is moving forward and just about everybody cares very much for the environment. You can believe what you hear in your country or you can come to America and see for yourself what I am talking about.

REAL MYTHS...

- Americans love soccer.
- Americans are never in a hurry.
- Americans don't like pick-up trucks.
- American households only have one television.
- Americans have short commutes to work.
- All Americans speak at least two languages.

HOST PARENT

24 - TWO BECOME ONE

It would be wrong if I said it is going to happen to you, but if it works out the way it should, your host family will become a real family to you. Of course not like your true family back home, but certainly one that you can call your "second" family. In our case I like to think that our exchange daughter views us as her second family, or at least as her American family. There is no doubt that we established a life-long bond that has proven to be strong well after her exchange year with us. We talk as often as possible, chat on the computer, send packages and even visit on vacations when possible. Most interesting is that our exchange daughter became a family member in her actions, attitudes and personality. After a short time it was as if she had always been part of the family. This was not just one sided as our family learned a lot from our exchange daughter as well. It is possible that you can gain more than an experience in American, very possibly a family too.

DID YOU KNOW?

Did you know that although the divorce rate in America is said to be around 50%, the American family is still strong. A popular quote by the well known American psychologist and advice columnist Dr. Joyce Brothers sums it up. *"When you look at your life, the greatest happiness's are family happiness's."* (14)

AMERICAN SLANG

I had "cold feet" about joining in the conversation at the first dinner with my host family. (This means you were scared or nervous.)

STATE of the UNION

South Carolina State Capital - Columbia

EXCHANGE STUDENT

24 - TWO BECOME ONE

It's true; you can really gain a second family during your exchange year in America. How close you become to your host family will depend on many things and if you don't fit in perfectly, it doesn't mean that you are going to have a bad time. Luckily it did happen to me and my host family has become my second family and I love them like my real family. Of course it wasn't like that from the first day. Becoming a family takes time, mixed with a little luck and a bunch of hard work. From day one my host parents treated me like their own children and I never felt like an outsider looking in. In return, I respected my host parents and listened to them like I would my own parents (hopefully better, as I'm sure my real mom would say). Although having host siblings is great, it does require even more work. Suddenly there was another kid in the house and the new kid is an intruder that now had needs and requirements too. This puts stress on the other siblings that requires patience and often there are differences. Acceptance comes with time and soon we became a new family. An outgoing American host family, who took in a shy German girl, made one unique family that had great fun for one glorious year.

TIPS...

- Be yourself. This is a new family for you, but over time it will become your family too.
- Follow the family rules and help with family chores.
- Participate in family activities. Do not hide in your bedroom or be shy about joining in family discussions and activities.
- Share your family stories and activities with your host family.

HOST PARENT

25 - HELLO and GOODBYE

Most of the time hellos are fun and goodbyes are sad, but whether you are just meeting your host family or just leaving them, both are going to be etched in your memory forever. You are going to be both excited and nervous when you leave for your airplane, so be ready for almost anything. After going through customs and grabbing your luggage you can start looking for your exchange counselor, or your host parents or your entire host family. Who knows what they may have planned for your first day, so be ready for just about anything. We let our exchange student unpack, unwind and just hang out as we all got to know each other a little bit. We learned a lot about each other and spent much time talking about our school and our city while our exchange daughter did the same. Other host families may have a small party for you to meet other family members or other friends that you may be seeing at school. Looking back at our experience, I truly enjoyed our first several days and weeks with our exchange daughter.

DID YOU KNOW?

Even though Paul McCartney of the Beatles said the song has absolutely no meaning, the Beatles hit titled "Hello Goodbye" works perfectly for our book. Hello and goodbye mean much more to an exchange student and a host family as summed up by the Beatles "You say goodbye and I say hello".

AMERICAN SLANG

"Mark my words," leaving your real family and your host family are both extremely difficult. (By saying this you are letting somebody know that you will be correct.)

STATE of the UNION

Michigan Nickname - Great Lakes State

EXCHANGE STUDENT

25 - HELLO and GOODBYE

Saying hello was exciting, but I was very nervous about meeting my new family and about speaking only English. Saying goodbye was extremely sad and I found out that it was much different than saying goodbye to your real family, because you don't really know if you will ever see your host family again. Before I left my home for America I had a goodbye party with all of my friends and when I left America at the end of my exchange year I had another goodbye party, but this time it was with all my new friends. I will admit that saying hello and goodbye to both of your families is like riding a rollercoaster. You feel up and down, excited and nervous...happy when it begins and sad when it ends. Yes, the week before you leave for America and the week before you leave for home are tough, but it is all part of the experience and you will get through it. The airport trips are the hardest because nobody wants to see you leave whether you are coming or going. Now that my year is long over I can say it was all worth it. Hellos and goodbyes are NOT forever. I e-mail and video chat with my host family and they have already visited me in Germany and I believe the hellos and goodbyes will be happening for a long time.

TIPS...

In America, like in your country, there are many different ways to say hello and goodbye. Try all of these:

Hello - Hi, Hi there, Howdy, Hey, Hey there, What's up, Sup (short for what's up), Hiya, Aloha (Hawaiian), What's happening

Goodbye - Bye, Bye-Bye (said quickly), See ya, See ya later, Later, Tah-Tah

Almost to America

Before you go…

Making gifts for friends

CHAPTER 2
AROUND THE HOUSE

HOST PARENT

26 - INTERNET

We all know that the Internet has changed the world in many ways, and it is no different for students and families participating in exchange programs. As an exchange student you no longer have to deal with time delayed post letters or expensive international rate phone calls. The Internet has made communication easy, fun and in real time. E-mails are received by your friends and family with photos and stories within minutes. Skype is a great software program used to communicate with family via a web cam making the international phone call obsolete. Although having a computer and Internet is not a requirement for being an exchange student, it really does make life as an exchange student and host family much easier. You will be able to experience life in America with your host family while remaining in close touch with your family back home. If your parents (real and host) do not speak the same language, you will have great fun watching them try to talk to each other. When you stop laughing you will need to help them.

DID YOU KNOW?

According to 2010 statistics, almost 25% of the world population utilizes the Internet with Europe at 48.9%, Asia at 17.4% and North America at 74.4%. (15)

AMERICAN SLANG

My computer crashed but my best friend is a computer "geek" and he can fix it. (Used to describe an intellectual person and recently associated with computer skills.)

EXCHANGE STUDENT

26 - INTERNET

You will be leaving your whole life behind you and you will not be seeing your family and friends in person for a long time. This does not mean that you cannot see them or talk to them. Actually, thanks to the Internet, it is now easier than ever. Your exchange organization will discourage you from talking to your family and friends too often because it could lead to homesickness. For me, I was able to have the best of both worlds. I would spend each week living the American life with my host family and on the weekend I would set a time with my real family to catch up on their life at home and my life abroad. The Internet, and in particular, programs like Skype, have made it possible to speak with my family and friends at no cost and with a web cam we can even see each other. It is also fun to involve your host family in your conversations and let them speak with your family. It is fun to watch them struggle to communicate, but a little frightening to listen to four parents all talking about you.

FACTS...

- A 2010 study reports that 53% of American households now subscribe to broadband Internet. (16)
- J.C.R. Licklider is widely credited with inventing the Internet while at the Massachusetts Institute of Technology. (17)

STATE of the UNION

Arkansas State Capital - Little Rock

HOST PARENT

27 - STEREOTYPES

Simply defined, stereotyping is when people categorize an individual based on their belonging to a certain class or group of people. Nobody is immune from stereotyping, including me, my family and our exchange student. You will probably stereotype your exchange student before you even meet him/her. This is primarily due to your lack of knowledge of their country, their culture and their personality. We quickly discovered that having an exchange student proved stereotyping as wrong and in many cases simply demeaning. I am not an "arrogant" American and my exchange student is not an "uptight" German...see what I mean? It's not true and not nice. Get to know as much as you can about your exchange student's culture, country and home. You will find your stereotype barriers falling before your eyes.

DID YOU KNOW?

The word stereotype is from the printing business used as a metaphor meaning that our "*imagination is shaped by the pictures seen* (in our head)" (18)

AMERICAN SLANG

I can tell by his accent that he's a "Yankee"! (A Yankee is a nickname for Americans used in many other countries.)

STATE of the UNION

Colorado Nickname - Colorful Colorado

EXCHANGE STUDENT

27 - STEREOTYPES

One of the most important things I learned as an exchange student in America is that stereotypes are very common, often mean and mostly untrue. Stereotypes are invented by people who think they know something about a person just by the group or culture to which they belong. As much as I did not want to believe it, I was influenced by a horrible stereotype that Americans were fat, stupid and lazy people. Like other countries that I have visited, I observed people that are fat, skinny, stupid, smart, lazy and highly motivated. But stereotypes are a two-way street and Americans are not immune to their own. One stereotype I actually found to be funny was that all of Germany is a Bavarian place with beer drinking, sausage eating people wearing lederhosen. Now as fun as that may sound, it is simply not true. No matter what country you come from, be prepared for many stereotypes and crazy questions about your country and your culture. Remember that you are here to learn and to help break down those barriers.

TIPS...

- Talk to your host family about stereotyping at school. Although it is typically harmless, it can be insulting and it will help to talk about it.
- Be prepared for more stereotyping than usual since many people may have predetermined opinions about your home country or culture.

HOST PARENT

28 - FAST FOOD

The rumors are true: fast food has become the worst enemy of America and American kids. The entire lifestyle in America is fast paced, hectic and busy. Students are often the busiest people in American families with school, sports, clubs and many other social activities. Fast food is convenient, inexpensive and can be found in every city and town no matter the size. Like it or not, fast food restaurants have become a part of our culture and landscape. There is hardly a town that does not have a McDonald's, Wendy's or Burger King. If that is not enough, you will possibly bump into an Arby's, Subway, Taco Bell or any number of "local" fast food restaurants. Fast food can be fun, but you should limit how much you eat just as American students should. Fast food is now offered in many school cafeterias ...packing a lunch is often the best option for your health and your budget.

DID YOU KNOW?

It is estimated that 1 in 4 Americans visit a fast food restaurant every day. (19) Based on current U.S. population estimates, this means approximately 75 million Americans eat a fast food meal every day.

AMERICAN SLANG

Who wants to go to McDonalds for "Take Out"? (In America, take out is when you take food away from the restaurant to eat at home or somewhere other than the restaurant.)

EXCHAGE STUDENT

28 - FAST FOOD

America = Fast Food, Fast Food = America. That is what I thought. That is what my friends thought. That is what I found to be true! Although I do not like stereotypes, this is one that cannot be denied. Even in the smaller towns (including where I lived) you could find several types of fast food establishments. It is so common that stopping to pick up a lunch or dinner is no big deal. If you decide to become an exchange student in America there is no way around seeing one, visiting one and adding a few extra pounds from one. If you do happen to avoid the local fast food restaurant you are not likely to avoid the fast food available in the school cafeteria. In fact, I highly recommend French fries. My friends and I would share a plate of "fries" every day at lunch, but don't worry, exercise took care of the extra calories.

TIPS...

- Most fast food restaurants now offer healthy choices. Make sure you check the entire menu for items such as salads and low fat meals.
- Never "Supersize" your meal which does nothing more than adds an extra helping of saturated fat and calories.

STATE of the UNION

Virginia State Capital - Richmond

HOST PARENT

29 - CHORES

You are certainly not thinking about becoming an exchange student to clean a house, wash a car and watch somebody's toddlers. If you are doing too many of these activities, then your host family has made a huge mistake. You are here for many reasons: to experience life in America, to experience a different culture, to continue your education, to make new international friends and hopefully to "adopt" a family for life. Unfortunately, chores are an important part of every kid's life and exchanges students must share in daily family responsibilities too. I am sure your life in America will be as busy as your life at home. As an American student your day will be filled with things like homework, practice and social activities. Regardless of all your activities, you will have time for your chores. Your chores will be assigned to you by your host parents and it will be your responsibility to fit them into your school and social schedule. Although helping the family is a good thing, keep in mind that you are an exchange student and not an au pair. If you feel that you have been given so many chores that you are unable to finish school work or participate in activities, then you should speak to your host parents about your concerns.

DID YOU KNOW?
Although we could not find proof during our research, it seems that among friends and family, all agree that the most unpopular chore is cleaning bathrooms and more specifically, cleaning toilets.

AMERICAN SLANG
"No sweat", I'll get my chores done by dinner time. (This means it should be easy or it will be no problem.)

EXCHANGE STUDENT

29 - CHORES

Who is going to do your laundry, wash your dishes, clean your bedroom, change your sheets and pack your lunch? Just think about how many things your mom and dad do that you take for granted. When you leave your real parents behind and begin an adventure with a new family, you will likely be doing some things you've never had to do before. In addition to your necessary daily tasks, you will likely be assigned a chore or two during your stay. I think it is important to share in the household responsibilities just like every other member of your host family. I was assigned dishwashing with my host brother and, of course, I was expected to keep my room looking respectable. Don't be afraid to ask your host parents for directions or help if you are asked to do something that is new to you or even to request a certain chore you may like to do.

TIPS...

Five things you can help your host family with:

- Laundry
- Setting table / Cleaning dishes
- Cleaning bathroom / your bedroom
- Vacuuming
- Shoveling snow / cutting grass

STATE of the UNION

South Dakota Nickname - Mount Rushmore State

HOST PARENT

30 - DRIVING

Host parents may be told that it is not their responsibility for your transportation, but is that the case with their own children? The fact of the matter is that the host parents should be willing to put in the same commitment to you as for any other family member. Most exchange students are not allowed to drive (this depends on your organization) and most do not even have a driver's license. America is huge and in most places throughout the county we do not have public transportation systems or certainly not any that match those of many other countries. Sure, you can take the bus back and forth to school, but that is only a small portion of the American experience. Sports teams, school clubs, theatre and musical groups are just some of the things that may take place well after the busses are parked for the night. Most of the time you will find that your host family is willing to make the commitment needed to get you around, but it would be wise to make a network of friends that are willing to ride-share so you can get where you want to be.

DID YOU KNOW?

Approximately 1 in 4 crash fatalities involve somebody 16 to 24 years old, so choose your ride carefully. (20)

AMERICAN SLANG

Abigail called "shotgun" before you did Dominique.

(The first person to yell shotgun gets to sit in the front seat of the vehicle.)

STATE of the UNION

North Carolina State Capital - Raleigh

EXCHANGE STUDENT

30 - DRIVING

Can you pick me up at such and such time? Can you take me to so and so's house? I really need a ride to practice. You will be using these phrases a lot as an exchange student in America because (most) exchange students are not allowed to drive. It is a weird feeling when all of your friends have cars and are able to drive, especially when many of them are younger than you. Transportation can be a difficult part of your experience in America because the distances can often be long and public transportation is poor to non-existent (unless you are living in a big city). You will need your host family and friends to get you around unless you want to spend your entire time in your school and at your host house. Most American families are used to this and are more than willing to accommodate you unless you take advantage of them and abuse the privileges. Follow their rules and requests regarding transportation and you should not have a problem getting to your destination.

FACTS...

- Most American kids get their driver's license when they turn 16.
- American cars are big and many people own large pick-up trucks.
- Many students drive their cars to school instead of taking the school bus.
- If you find that you are taking rides from one or two friends regularly, offer to pay for gasoline occasionally; it will be greatly appreciated.

HOST PARENT

31 - PEANUT BUTTER and JELLY

I grew up on peanut butter and jelly sandwiches, but our exchange student did not. After meeting exchange students from all over the world, I am beginning to believe that peanut butter and jelly sandwiches are only popular in America. In college we did not want to stop eating peanut butter and jelly sandwiches so we just made it sound "cool" by calling them PB&Js, which is now common slang for this popular sandwich. You will find many new foods besides PB&J that you will enjoy and several foods that you will find disgusting. We have found that the different foods we eat are a great way to share cultural differences and experience new tastes. Your host family will find it fun to think of foods that you have never tried and even more fun for you to share some of your foods with your host family. Bon Appétit.

DID YOU KNOW?

It is estimated that by the time a student graduates from high school they will have eaten 1,500 peanut butter and jelly sandwiches. (21)

AMERICAN SLANG

I'll be there in a "jiffy"; I'm just making a PB&J for lunch.
(You will be there fast or quick.)

STATE of the UNION

Maryland Nickname - Old Line State

EXCHANGE STUDENT

31 - PEANUT BUTTER and JELLY

If I didn't know better, I would say that peanut butter is an entire "food group" in the United States. In America, peanut butter is everywhere—peanut butter (& jelly) sandwiches for lunch, peanut butter crackers for snacks, peanut butter cookies for dessert and even peanut butter toast for breakfast. The U.S.A. is PB&J CRAZY. Did you know that they even spread peanut butter on celery, and then load it with raisins and they actually named it "Ants on a Log"? Wow, if only I liked peanut butter. Finally, just to drive my point home, the Americans even have a popular song called...yes, you guessed it, *Peanut Butter and Jelly Time*. Now that is one type of peanut butter and jelly that I really liked. But if that is not enough for you, try their Sloppy Joes, Coney dogs, corn dogs, elephant ears and churros (or whatever regional foods you may find in your American state). I'll let you find about those all on your own, but make sure you don't miss out because they are all truly American surprises.

FACTS...

- Former US President Jimmy Carter spent much of his life in the peanut business.
- Peanuts are eaten raw, boiled and roasted.
- You can buy peanut butter and jelly premixed in a jar at the grocery store.
- Peanut butter comes in a smooth variety or chunky. Chunky is when actual pieces of peanuts are found in your peanut butter.
- Food is one of the best topics for breaking culture barriers. We all love to eat and we love to talk about eating.

HOST PARENT

32 - SIBLINGS

You may or may not have a host brother or sister and maybe you will have several. No matter what the ages of your host siblings, you will find it fun, rewarding and even helpful (particularly if they are near your age). Sure, you can learn a lot from your host parents and, sure, they care about your well-being, but a host sibling can be a true fiend and a person you can count on to get you through those first several difficult days and weeks. Our own kids helped our exchange daughter at school by introducing her to their friends, helping find her classrooms, sharing with her chores, helping with her homework or just being there to watch a movie or share a funny moment. Yes, you may argue a little or get a little jealous now and then, but if you get the chance to have a host sibling you may just have another brother or sister for the rest of your life. Patience is also important since getting a new sibling "overnight" may be difficult at first. Although our daughter and our exchange daughter took a long time to become true friends, they have become more than friends and are truly sisters!

DID YOU KNOW?

According to the U.S. Census bureau there are approximately 73.5 million Americans under the age of 18 so your chances of having a host sibling are pretty darn good. (22)

AMERICAN SLANG

My host brother is such a "pain in the neck"! (He's always causing trouble and bothering me.)

EXCHANGE STUDENT

32 - SIBLINGS

Before my exchange trip I had one little sister and now I have two little sisters and one big brother. That's right, when I walked through the gate at the airport I was greeted by my two American siblings. At first they seemed like two new friends that I was just getting to know, but I soon found out that they were to be more than friends. They would become real siblings. It is not always easy, but that is part of being a sibling and part of being a family. Siblings are also incredibly helpful in getting adjusted to American life and introducing you to many new friends. Just like at your real home you will spend a fair amount of time with your siblings at meals, on vacations, at school functions, at family activities and much more. Don't forget that you will share your whole life with them for almost a year, so you really will become close. I am glad I had host siblings, we became great friends and they will always be my little sister and older brother.

TIPS...

The number one factor influencing personality is birth order. The following are some interesting birth order traits:

- Firstborns are usually dominant and organized.
- It is said that middleborns have more romantic potential.
- Lastborns are typically friendly, easygoing and creative. (23)

STATE of the UNION

Indiana State Capital - Indianapolis

HOST PARENT

33 - DINNER

This topic was at the request of our exchange student, although I believe her interest may be very unique to our family. However, this does offer the opportunity to explain American meal times, which I had always assumed were universal. In America, breakfast is usually a rush before school and work while lunch is typically around 12:00 p.m. (noon) and dinner (or supper) is around 5:00 p.m. Except for breakfast, the other two meals are usually fairly large and often times (because of work schedules, work locations and students activities) dinner can be as late as 7:00 p.m. or 8:00 p.m.—this may explain why some of us are a little on the "large" size. Although it does not happen as much as I would like, when we all get to sit down for a family dinner together, it becomes my favorite time of the day. It is time to discuss what happened during the day, and for me, a time to joke around, laugh and enjoy each other's company.

DID YOU KNOW?

It all depends on where you live in America, but, generally speaking, most Americans use the words dinner and supper interchangeably. Some may argue that supper is a "lighter" dinner or that lunch may also be a supper. If you are confused it is best to just use breakfast, lunch and dinner.

AMERICAN SLANG

I can't wait to get home and have some "grub". (Grub is just another way of saying food.)

EXCHANGE STUDENT

33 - DINNER

Dinner time at my host house was crazy, loud, quiet, simple, extravagant, quick, long, sometimes absent and always FUN! That's right, I never knew what to expect, mostly because there were five of us all on different schedules and all in different moods. No matter who had a great day or who had a bad day, my host family found this to be the one time of the day to tell stories, make jokes and have fun. I enjoyed just about every minute of our dinner time together. Of course I cannot tell you how your host family will be during dinner, but I did get to share dinner with several other families and found one common trait: sharing the day's activities with each other. As my host dad already explained, dinner (and lunch) times are probably different than what you may be used to, but you will quickly get into the American daily routine.

FACTS...

- A BLT is a popular sandwich made of bacon, lettuce and tomato.
- A Root Beer Float is a drink made with vanilla ice cream and root beer soda (root beer is a soda that most exchange students have never tried). If you don't like the root beer then try it with ginger ale.
- A Sloppy Joe is a sandwich made with seasoned loose beef.
- A Coney Dog or Chili Dog is a hot dog covered in chili, mustard and onions.

STATE of the UNION

Nebraska Nickname - Cornhusker State

HOST PARENT

34 - PETS

Sampson, Felix and Zen are the masters of our house (or at least they think so). We have a "typical" American household of dogs and cats. Many families have pets and almost all have either one dog or cat. According to the American Pet Products Manufacturers Association (APPMA), 39% of US households have at least one dog and 34% of U.S. households have at least one cat (2007-2008 figures). This means that you have a pretty good chance of staying with an exchange family who owns a pet or two. Most pet owners feel that having a pet enhances their life and provides a needed companionship. If you are not allergic to animals then you may be lucky enough to have an exchange pet. Our exchange student does not have pets at home and our furry creatures fell helplessly in love with her...and I believe she had a little love in return.

FACTS...

The top 3 dog breeds are in America are: Labrador Retrievers, German Shepherds and Yorkshire Terriers. (24)

TERMS...

- Calico Cat - A cat with red, black, chocolate or cinnamon colors, usually a female cat.
- Tomcat (or Tom) - A Male cat is a Tomcat.
- Purr - The word used to describe the sound of a happy cat.

AMERICAN SLANG

My best friend has a poodle, but all we have is a "mutt".

(A mixed breed dog sometimes used just to describe a dog without a pedigree.)

EXCHANGE STUDENT

34 - PETS

Before I came to America I had never shared my house with an indoor pet (not counting a goldfish now and again). One of my best friends was told it was going to be hard to find a host family for her because of her allergies. We just couldn't believe how that could be true in such a huge country like the United States. After spending almost a year in America I have found that statement to be true. It seems like almost every family has at least one dog or cat and many have more. My host family had one huge dog and two bossy cats. Knowing in advance that my host family had pets, I was a little concerned that it was a part of daily life that I might not like. As it turns out I enjoyed it very much and I believe I will miss my host pets as much as my host family and I actually think the pets are going to miss me. If you have similar concerns you should forget about them right now. You will enjoy making a new canine or feline friend except when they wake you up in the middle of the night because they are crying in the hallway wanting to get into your bedroom and snuggle up into your warm bed.

DID YOU KNOW?
The most popular dog names in 2010 were: Buddy, Max, Daily, Bella, Lucy, Jack, Molly, Charlie, Sadie and Rocky. The most popular cat names in 2010 were: Lucy, Midnight, Bella, Molly, Smokey, Tiger, Oreo, Max, Princess and Charlie. (25)

STATE of the UNION
California State Capital - Sacramento

HOST PARENT

35 - RELIGION

The very first Europeans arrived on the shores of North America because of religious persecution in their own country. The Puritans (Pilgrims) were the first to arrive in 1620, but not the last. Other religions such as Catholic, Quaker, Jewish, Mormon, Amish and many forms of protestant religions are practiced in America. The United States was one of the first countries to make a distinct separation of church and state and most Americans are adamant about keeping the separation. Although America is a highly religious country, it is also extremely diverse and you will find almost any religion you want. You will also find that there is a lot of tolerance between religions and most Americans get along with each other no matter what religion they practice or don't practice. Feel free to attend a church that you may belong to or try something new—most everybody will welcome you to their church community.

DID YOU KNOW?

Currently the top five religions in America are: Catholic, Southern Baptist, United Methodist, Church of Jesus Christ of Latter-day Saints (Mormon) and The Church of God in Christ. (26)

AMERICAN SLANG

Some people are very "straight laced". (This is somebody who always follows the rules and uses the correct behavior and is often associated with very religious people.)

STATE of the UNION

Iowa Nickname - Hawkeye State

EXCHANGE STUDENT

35 - RELIGION

During my orientation and during yours, you will be informed that Americans are very religious. In comparison to my home country this is true, but just like everything else discussed in this book, it will obviously depend on your host family. Although my host family was Christian, they did not attend church regularly like many families I met during my stay in America. Some people attend service once every week while others attend twice a week or even more. Most churches have many activities other than worship services and almost all churches have youth groups. Church youth groups are a lot of fun and are just another way you can hang out with your current friends and a great opportunity to meet new friends from other schools and communities. Most of these youth groups meet weekly and often have functions and field trips that can be fun to attend. Don't get caught up worrying about religion before you leave, I am sure you will have fun no matter what the level of participation of your host family and no matter what religion they may be.

TIPS...

- Dress can be formal or casual depending on the church. Ask before you go.
- Arriving late or leaving early is discouraged.
- Do not bring your cell phone to church or turn it off before service begins.
- Many churches have modern services or services more directed toward young people.

HOST PARENT

36 - DREAMING

Dreams are images and feelings we have while we are sleeping but "dreaming" can also be defined as personal aspirations or individual goals. Maybe you have always dreamed of becoming an exchange student as I have always dreamed of writing a book. This book is a culmination of both those dreams, that of my exchange daughter and my own. Being an exchange student is a big event in your life and once you live this dream you will find that many of your other dreams are possible and your eyes will be opened to limitless possibilities. Walt Disney said *"All our dreams can come true, if we have the courage to pursue them"*. Your courage to complete this dream is the beginning to your understanding that all dreams can become reality when the dream is something you really want.

DID YOU KNOW?

One of Sigmund Freud's most famous books titled *The Interpretation of Dreams* was an important book in its time. Freud believed that we repress our urges and impulses in a civilized society and that we release these feelings in our dreams.

AMERICAN SLANG

I was so tired after school that I took a "catnap".

(Cats sleep a lot and this mean a short afternoon nap just like your cat might take.)

STATE of the UNION

Washington State Capital - Olympia

EXCHANGE STUDENT

36 - DREAMING

The first several weeks you spend in America you will probably dream about home and about what experiences you have already had at your new home and your new school. It is not a surprise to you that you will be speaking English in America, but would you be surprised if I tell you that you will also dream in English? Now that you are speaking English every day, your host family is speaking English and all your new friends are speaking English, it only seems natural that you will dream in English. You would have to agree that since your whole life is being lived in English, it would be a little strange if your host family and American friends were speaking your native language. Sometimes you will find yourself dreaming in both languages and you might even find your American friends speaking your native language and your friends from home speaking English... don't ask me why, it's only a dream.

FACTS...

Can these be true?

You are paralyzed while you sleep

- Everybody dreams
- You forget 90% of your dreams
- Blind people dream
- Not everybody dreams in color
- You may soon be dreaming in English (27)

HOST PARENT

37 - POLITICS

In America we have elephants and donkeys and I'm not talking about animals in the zoo. Yes, I am actually speaking politics, American style. Those are the mascots of the two major political parties in America—elephants are Republicans and donkeys are Democrats. In regards to political agendas it is well known that Republicans are considered conservative, while Democrats are liberal in their views. Maybe you will be lucky enough to be here during a presidential election year which happens every four years and sometimes feels like a sporting event with the crazy television coverage. In recent years, many Americans have become frustrated with politics because of the negative campaigning that takes place between these two main political parties. Regardless of which animal your host family votes for, it is not likely that politics will be a subject that will influence your stay in America. At the very least, you may find American politics interesting or even entertaining.

DID YOU KNOW?

America has almost always had a two-party system. After the Revolutionary War it was the Republicans and the Whigs later followed by the Whigs and the Democrats and now the Democrats and the Republicans...not to be confused with the original Republicans.

AMERICAN SLANG

The Presidency was "up for grabs". (This means it is a close race and anybody may win.)

EXCHANGE STUDENT

37 - POLITICS

The term of a U.S. President is four years and I was fortunate enough to be an exchange student during one of the most interesting and historic elections in American history. I was in America for the election of the first African American U.S. President, Barak Obama. This election and the several months leading up to the election was a crazy time period. Political signs, television commercials, news programs and daily conversations were all about the election and everybody was debating this topic and that topic. People were either Democrats or Republicans and there were differences of opinions even within households. Even students at school talked about the elections and debated on who was the better candidate. My host mom took to me to the voting station and I was able to truly witness the election first hand. After all the arguing and all the "politics", it was fun to watch. In the end, everything became normal again and everybody got along just fine.

FACTS...

- Each U.S. State has two elected Senators.
- Each U.S. State is allowed a certain number of Representatives based on each State's population.
- The U.S. Supreme Court has nine judges appointed for life. Appointments are made by the President.

STATE of the UNION

Idaho Nickname - Gem State

HOST PARENT

38 - RULES

I would always tease my exchange daughter by telling her that Germans are "rule followers" and that Americans are "rule breakers". This is not actually true and I'm stereotyping, which as I earlier said, was not a good thing to do. The truth is that rules are important and just like at your real home you will also have rules in your exchange home. Many of these rules will be the same, but some of them may be different. This is because you are in a different country where the culture has created different standards than your own. This is one of the main reasons you are starting this journey. You are with a different family that will have different standards, opinions and, you guessed it...rules. Rules are important and you should respect the rules of your host family or your year may not be as perfect as you were expecting. If you think something is unfair or against your beliefs, then go ahead and discuss your concerns with your host parents. They are people too, and a good discussion may just clear up your concerns.

DID YOU KNOW?

You can't play a game without rules. Try to play a board game that you have never seen before and do not read the rules. You will find that the only way to play and the only way somebody can win is if you make up your own rules.

AMERICAN SLANG

If you don't follow the rules you are going to find yourself in the "dog house". (This is another way of saying that you or somebody is in trouble.)

STATE of the UNION

Kentucky State Capital - Frankfort

EXCHANGE STUDENT

38 - RULES

Being an exchange student includes having a lot of rules that you are expected to follow. This is not any different than following rules at home, but now you are in a different country and living with a different family. There are rules from your exchange organization, rules from your host country, rules from your school, and of course, rules from your host family. Many of these rules will be provided to you in some form of writing or in an orientation class, but there are also many "unwritten" (or untold) rules that you need to keep in mind. Your host family decided to give you a home for a couple months and of course they do not expect you to do hard labor for them, but you have to be nice and follow some of these polite rules. You should know these from your own home and you should follow them all the times, not just during your exchange year. They include general things like being nice; asking if someone needs help and thanking somebody for something they have done for you. Follow these and other common sense rules and you will be a fine representative of your country.

TIPS...

- You will not be allowed to be a passenger in a vehicle driven by a student with a learning permit (unless a driver over 21 is in vehicle)
- Alcohol drinking is not allowed in the U.S. until you are 21 years old.
- Skipping school without your host parent's permission will get you in trouble at school and home.

HOST PARENT

39 - PRIVACY and MODESTY

You will not need to worry about privacy during your stay in America. I do not want to stereotype my fellow Americans, but I would not be completely wrong to say that most Americans are modest, conservative and private when compared to many other countries around the world. You will not see shared (men's/women's) restrooms, public breastfeeding or nudity of any kind in the United States (including broadcast television). This will be the standard in your American home and you will most likely have your own private bedroom and possibly your own bathroom. It may almost seem funny sometimes when you see people get so bothered by public displays of affection or if somebody shows a little too much skin. You can feel good knowing that your privacy in America will be guaranteed and you will not need to worry about finding a private place to call your own and to slip away for a little while from your temporary American lifestyle.

DID YOU KNOW?

American's are so concerned about privacy that during routine doctor or hospital exams you are given a paper robe, privacy curtains and you never uncover until the last possible moment.

AMERICAN SLANG

If you don't close the bathroom door somebody might see you in the "buff". (It typically means somebody is naked, but it is also what American's call somebody with big muscles.)

EXCHANGE STUDENT

39 - PRIVACY and MODESTY

Everybody has a bad day once in a while and for me it is times like this when I need a little privacy. If needed, I could always find privacy in my bedroom or I could take a walk through the woods to think about my concerns and work out my problems. It was not difficult to get used to American modesty and conservative views. It is their culture and it is important to remember that learning and living their culture is partly why you are taking this trip. On the other hand, don't take this topic too seriously either; because it is not as bad as my host dad has made it sound (I think my host dad inherited many of his traits from his European ancestors). Your biggest change may be the rules at school that require everybody to wear proper clothing. If you don't follow what I call "school modesty rules" (outlined in the tips section) then you will either be sent home or they will make you put on something that is allowed, and who wants to call their host parents and ask them to bring more "appropriate" clothing to school?

TIPS...

Most schools have modesty dress codes. Here are a couple rules you may find at your new American school:

- Shorts or skirts must be no shorter than your knee (no shorter than finger-tip length when your arms are hanging to your sides).
- Sleeves on shirts must be at least three fingers wide.
- No clothing with profanity or nudity is allowed.

STATE of the UNION

Delaware Nickname - First State

HOST PARENT

40 - HOMEWORK

In American high school you are going to have a different teacher every hour for six or seven hours a day. You will quickly learn that each teacher is different, including their views on homework. Some teachers assign a lot of homework while others do not. Some teachers allow enough time to get the work done in class. One thing is a guarantee...you will have special projects in many classes that will require extra hours at home in order to get them done. For example, you may have to write a short story for a creative writing class, a video for your Spanish class or prepare an experiment at home for your biology class. Keep in mind that you will still be required to complete homework on time even if you have soccer practice, drama practice or a club meeting. Homework assignments are always a large part of your grade. If you want to truly enjoy your time at home and school, then get your homework done every day.

DID YOU KNOW?

By reading this book you are already way ahead of many others because you are doing your homework necessary for a successful exchange year in America. Good luck and keep reading.

AMERICAN SLANG

Having this much homework is such a "drag". (If it's a drag it is disappointing, depressing and not fun. You could also say bummer or downer.)

STATE of the UNION

Georgia State Capital - Atlanta

EXCHANGE STUDENT

40 - HOMEWORK

During your exchange year you are going to be a normal American student and the teachers will probably treat you like one. This means you have to do everything that your American classmates have to do, including homework. For me, homework at my American high school was a lot easier than the homework I would typically get in my home country of Germany. In my American high school we only have six classes and we usually had enough time to get our work done in class, but occasionally I would have to finish longer assignments at home. There is one important fact that you should know about homework at high school in America: for every assignment you complete you will receive points, and the more points you get then the better your grade will be. Homework does not always have to be boring; it can be a lot of fun. For example, one day I had to learn all 50 American States and I asked my host family for help. We had a great time reviewing them as they gave me tips (and even songs) to help remember them. By the way, I got them all correct on my geography test.

TIPS...

- When you get home from school, take a quick break but before you do anything else - get your homework done.
- Never wait till Sunday night to finish your weekend homework.
- If you have host siblings then share homework time together and it will make homework more fun.
- Turn off you Internet chat so you are not disturbed and you can concentrate on completing your homework.

HOST PARENT

41 - NEIGHBORHOODS and HOMES

If you've ever seen an American movie, than you may already be familiar with a typical U.S. home and neighborhood. On the other hand, America is so big and climates are so varied (depending on where you will be living), that you will find homes are different as well. In the colder climates, most homes are made of wood, brick or even logs while in the warmer climates, homes will be made of stucco (plaster) and brick. Unless you live on a farm in the country, you will most likely live in a neighborhood (often called subdivisions as you get closer and closer to big cities) with a certain amount of other homes similar to your own. Home sizes and yard sizes are obviously dependent on income levels, but most homes range between 1,000 sf and 3,000 sf (93 m^2 to 278 m^2) and have between two and five bedrooms. Once you get your street address for your new exchange home don't waste any time checking it out on *Google Earth*. You will easily be able to look at your new neighborhood, house and maybe you can even find your new school.

DID YOU KNOW?

In some American neighborhoods homeowners are required to join the neighborhood association. The yearly association fees pay for services conducted in the neighborhood such as snow plowing, grass cutting or the neighborhood recreation center (if they have one).

AMERICAN SLANG

My host family has the coolest "crib". (This is a cool term for a house or your home but it really means a bed that a baby sleeps in.)

STATE of the UNION

Mississippi Nickname - Magnolia State

EXCHANGE STUDENT

41 - NEIGHBORHOODS and HOMES

Everybody has seen an American movie, which means most of you have seen a typical American home and neighborhood. Actually, I never paid too much attention to them while watching these movies, but when I saw my American home for the first time I felt like I was living right in a movie. I noticed a big difference between houses and neighborhoods in the United States from those I am familiar with in Europe. It is difficult to describe all of them, but there are some obvious differences. In my small German town houses are further apart, they are made of mostly brick and they don't look exactly the same like many in American neighborhoods. I also found it very interesting that it is no big deal for American families to move to another part of the country not only because they have to, but sometimes, just because they feel like it. I suppose it is possible it could happen during your stay, but probably not and who knows, maybe you'll move from the snow in North Dakota to the sunshine in southern California. You may even move next door to a movie star. Oops, now I'm dreaming and that is entirely another topic.

TIPS...

- Americans move a lot. It is no big deal for an American family to live in Ohio this year and Virginia next year.
- American relatives are often separated by many miles with a brother living in New York and a sister living in California.
- It is very common to find empty homes with both parents away at work and kids at school.

HOST PARENT

42 - CITY, 'BURBS or STICKS

America has something for everybody, whether you want to live on a farm, live in a beautiful neighborhood, or even if you want to live in a high-rise apartment in a big city like New York or Chicago. Keeping that in mind, it is generally believed that over fifty percent of U.S. citizens live in the suburbs. The suburbs are a creation of the continued population growth and the expansion of big cities and neighborhoods away from the city center (commonly referred to as urban sprawl). Although you may live on a farm or in the country, it is most likely that you will end up living in the suburbs with the majority of us Americans. Don't worry, America has been built around this suburbia and you will find plenty of malls, restaurants, movie theatres and parks where you can still experience what has become popularly described as "small-town America".

DID YOU KNOW?

The U.S. population has grown from 76 million in 1900 to 281 million in 2000. The population has increased approximately 1.3% a year in the 20th century while many other countries are actually having a decline in population. This is the main reason for the growth of suburban America. (28)

AMERICAN SLANG

We live way out in the "boonies". (When you live in the country, away from the city then you live in the "middle of nowhere" or in the boonies.)

STATE of the UNION

Montana State Capital - Helena

EXCHANGE STUDENT

42 - CITY, 'BURBS or STICKS

What that heck is my host dad talking about? Isn't learning English hard enough without having to learn made up slang words like 'burbs and sticks? I now know that what he means is that you can find all kinds of cities in America: small, medium or big. Because my home is in a small village, I was most impressed with the big cities like Chicago and Washington D.C., but my American home town was a mixture of a big city suburb and what is known as "small town America". Since America is different than your country, you will find that you will like just about anywhere that you are placed, but most likely you will be in what is called a suburban neighborhood. Homes will be fairly close to each other, they will look similar and they will be located on uniquely named American streets like Kennedy, Mayflower or Gettysburg. Half of the fun is finding out where you are going to live and you are going to love your American home whether you live on a farm, in the sticks, or in a modern home in the 'burbs.

FACTS...

- A group of homes built at a similar time and often by the same builder is called a neighborhood. American slang: "hood"
- Another word used for neighborhood is subdivision. American slang: "sub"
- As a large city grows, homes expand further and further away from the city into new cities all categorized as the suburbs. American slang: "'burbs"
- Most Americans living in the country are said to be living in the "sticks" (rural area surrounded by trees).

HOST PARENT

43 - JUNK FOOD and SNACKS

Americans love junk food (or at least that is what we are constantly told in the media). It appears that this may be true based on a report by the International Obesity Task Force that identifies the United State as having over 30% of its adults classified as obese. Obesity in American children is growing at an alarming rate and all of this adds up to a lack of exercise and too much junk food. I classify junk food as not only snacks (like potato chips or candy) but also fast food like hamburgers, doughnuts or submarine sandwiches. During your stay in America you will be overwhelmed with your choices of junk food and snacks available at many homes and at many schools. Be warned, like many Americans, once you start down the road of junk food addiction, it is difficult to stop. This does not mean that you should completely avoid junk food, only that you should not make it your main source of nutrition during your year in the U.S.A. By the way, make sure you have some Reese's Pieces candy, they are my favorite.

DID YOU KNOW?

A 2004 movie titled *Super Size Me* is a documentary film showing what happens to a person who does not exercise and eats nothing but McDonalds for breakfast, lunch and dinner every day for 30 days. The results are interesting, horrifying and predictable. Check it out.

AMERICAN SLANG

When I get home from school I always have the "munchies". (If you have the munchies, you are hungry for a snack.)

STATE of the UNION

North Dakota Nickname - Peace Garden State

EXCHANGE STUDENT

43 - JUNK FOOD and SNACKS

You will eat a lot of junk food in the United States, even when you promise your parents that you won't eat all that unhealthy stuff while you are gone. There is no way around it. Sure, we have a lot of junk food in my country as well, but there seems to be a lot more in America. You will pack junk food in your lunch, you will find junk food in the school cafeteria and sometimes you will buy it at a fast food restaurant. Worst of all, you may have it for breakfast, lunch and dinner. At school you will also find vending machines that sell drinks and of course more junk food in case you get hungry after school or you forget to bring your lunch. At a party you won't even be able to try all the different kinds of junk food that will be available. Your trip to America will include pizza, cookies, brownies, pop, chips, salsa, ice cream and tons of other unhealthy foods. Even though it is not good for you, you must try them all because some of them are incredibly delicious. My favorite junk food is cookies, especially chocolate chip cookies right out of the oven. Cookies are everywhere in America and they are so good.

FACTS...

After considerable research we have found that everybody has a different list of what are considered the worst snack foods. Some snacks that come up on almost everybody's list are:

Potato Chips	Soda (Pop)
French Fries	Pizza
Cookies	Candy
Donuts	Onion Rings

HOST PARENT

44 - SMOKING and DRINKING

These are a couple of sensitive subjects in the United States and they deserve some discussion so you do not find yourself making a mistake during your stay. I'll tackle the subject of smoking and let my exchange daughter provide you with the information about drinking. The government and various health organizations have worked hard at reducing the number of smokers in the U.S. For example, most public buildings (including restaurants) do not allow smoking or have designated smoking areas and there is much advertising to educate the public on the health risks associated with this habit. Their efforts have been successful and the American Center for Disease Control (CDC) reports the number of smokers is below 20% for the first time ever. Unfortunately, because of peer pressure, many kids still smoke in America and cigarettes are easy to get. Most States require you to be 18 years old to purchase tobacco products and no school allows cigarette smoking in their buildings. Some states, like ours, can even write you a ticket if you are caught smoking anywhere on school property (including in your car).

DID YOU KNOW?

Every year the American Cancer Society promotes their "Great American Smokeout Challenge". The Smokeout begins on the third Thursday of each November and encourages smokers to quit and provides many assistance tools to help get the job done.

AMERICAN SLANG

I left the party because underage kids were drinking "booze". (Booze is another work for alcoholic drinks.)

STATE of the UNION

Tennessee State Capital - Nashville

EXCHANGE STUDENT

44 - SMOKING and DRINKING

Like my host dad said, drinking is a sensitive subject in the U.S., but I am pretty sure a lot of you are interested in hearing about it from an exchange student. The legal drinking age in my country is 16 and to be completely honest, most of my friends like to drink alcohol once in a while. In America it is much different; you have to be 21 years old to legally drink alcohol and many teenagers in America have never had an alcoholic drink. If you decide to become an exchange student you have to be aware of the fact that you won't be able to drink for the entire time. If you decide to drink at parties where it is available, just remember that it is prohibited by law and it is not allowed by your exchange organization. American society and the police take underage drinking seriously and you may even be arrested if caught. I can honestly say that I had as much fun (and maybe more fun) at my American parties with no alcoholic drinks than those at home where sometimes drinking would cause a few people to get a bit too crazy.

TIPS...

- Don't let your friends at parties talk you into drinking alcohol while in America. Respect the laws and rules you are required to follow while in America.
- Never accept a ride from somebody that you know has been drinking alcoholic drinks.
- Stay away from parties where you know in advance they will be serving alcoholic drinks.
- Do not smoke at school or home at any time.
- Try not to make friends that routinely break the law and will get you sent back to your real home early.

HOST PARENT

45 - GRANDPARENTS and FAMILY

Everybody loves their grandparents no matter what country you call home. They are always there to support you during each small achievement, they celebrate your birthdays, they give you a hug at just the right moment and they are always slipping money in your hand just when you ran out of your own. Now here is the best surprise of your exchange visit...you are about to get some host grandparents who are probably going to treat you just as good as your own and you can never have too many grandparents. Like your own grandparents (in case you don't already know), they have so much to offer in regards to your cultural experience. Grandparents have a rich history and a full life of American experiences that they will be willing to share with you and all you have to do is show a little interest. Don't forget you will not only be staying with a family but you will be included into the entire extended family which will include aunts, uncles, cousins and many others. Buckle up and be ready to jump into an American life with your entire American host family.

DID YOU KNOW?

National Grandparents day is celebrated on the first Sunday after Labor Day. Jimmy Carter, the 39th President of America began this celebration and stated that "*...They bore the hardships and made the sacrifices that produced much of the progress and comfort we enjoy today. It is appropriate, therefore, that as individuals and as a nation, that we salute our grandparents for their contribution to our lives.* (29)

AMERICAN SLANG

It was mean calling the man "over-the-hill". (You're old.)

STATE of the UNION

Massachusetts Nickname - Bay State

EXCHANGE STUDENT

45 - GRANDPARENTS and FAMILY

You will spend a lot of time with your host family, but your host family includes more than parents and siblings. There are also host grandparents, aunts, uncles, cousins and other relatives. Just like at home, your host family will celebrate holidays together which means you will get to know them well and you may spend a fair amount of time with them. When you first meet them they will ask you a lot of questions just like everyone you meet, but they will also welcome you as another part of the family. Talk to them and be friendly, because they are a part of your exchange year that you will enjoy very much. It can be a lot of fun to meet the extended family and to be included in their gatherings. We always played "Apples to Apples" which is a fun English word game and guess who always won? That's right; the German exchange student (me) was unbeatable! Like home, Grandparents are special and they make it so easy to build a special relationship with them. My host grandparents treated me like their own grandchild and they will always be in my memories. Remember, you can never have too many grandparents.

TIPS...

- Most American's call their grandparents Grandma and Grandpa but you will find many variations such as Nanny and Papa or even fun nicknames like G-ma and G-pa. They will want you to address them the same as their grandchildren.
- Talk to them and ask many questions. Most grandparents (like your own) love to talk about their family and their past.

HOST PARENT

46 - COOKING and BAKING

Every culture has great food and you will find great cooks in every country. As a matter of fact, many people enjoy traveling around the world just to experience these different tastes. You are not only going to have many opportunities to eat American foods, but you will have plenty of time to do some of your own baking and cooking. Like in your own country, holidays are a great time to help cook a festive dinner or to learn how to cook your new favorite cookies. Cooking is not only a way to spend some time, but it may be of great help to your host family during the busy holiday seasons or during a hectic week. On several occasions our exchange daughter cooked some traditional German dishes for dinner and it provided our family with some new foods as well. You will find many opportunities to cook dinner or bake a cake. You find this a fun way to spend some of your free time with your friends or your host family members.

DID YOU KNOW?

Most American families (with small children) leave a small plate full of freshly baked cookies and a large glass of milk for Santa Claus on Christmas Eve. Sugar cookies are the most popular Christmas cookies baked in holiday shapes and colors.

AMERICAN SLANG

My host-Grandma makes the most "yummy" chocolate chip cookies.
(Those cookies must be delicious or great tasting.)

STATE of the UNION

New Jersey State Capital - Trenton

EXCHANGE STUDENT

46 - COOKING and BAKING

I really love to cook and bake at home and I loved cooking with my host mom and sister too. Before I left Germany I thought I could cook a lot of my favorite German dishes for my host family in America, but when I finally found the time, it turned out to be a bigger challenge than I expected. First, you have to find all the ingredients, which turned out to be difficult in America, and second, you have to convert all the measurements out of the metric system. Instead of grams and milliliters, you will be using cups and ounces. Don't worry, it's not impossible to cook your favorite dish, but it will probably take longer than usual. You will also get to know your host families favorite dishes and then you can surprise your family at home with new dishes you have learned in America. Now I have two tips for you: 1.) Organize an international food party and cook your favorite dish from home. 2.) Bake a birthday cake for your best friend and bring it to school to share at lunch. These things will not only be fun to do, but your friends will love it too.

FACTS...

It is difficult to list typical American foods but here are several that you will find often during your stay:

COOKING	BAKING
Hamburgers/Hotdogs	Apple/Pumpkin Pies
Pizza/Pasta/Spaghetti	Cookies
Corn on the Cob	Brownies
Fried Chicken	Cupcakes
Macaroni and Cheese	Muffins
French Fries	Cobblers

HOST PARENT

47 - FAMILY SCHEDULES

If you like to participate in activities other than school work, then you are going to need a schedule. If you have host siblings, then you are going to need a bigger schedule, and if both of your host parents work, then you may need a very big family schedule. What's the big deal and why do we need this topic? As you read through this book you will discover that:

1. Many American families have both parents working outside of the home.
2. Sports and clubs are typically conducted before or after school and school busses do not provide transportation to or from these events.
3. There is typically poor public transportation in most cities and only a few kids drive to school.
4. Extra siblings translate to more events and it complicates the transportation issues.

It will be absolutely necessary for you to communicate and be involved in the family scheduling so you can get where you want to be, when you want to be there. Your host parents want to help, but you will also need to help, so spend the extra time to work on your schedules.

DID YOU KNOW?

Most American kids are overscheduled and their parents are often running all over just to get them to their activities. Many kids leave at 6:30 and do not return until 10:00.

AMERICAN SLANG

Our schedule didn't work so it's "back to the drawing board". (This means to start all over again.)

STATE of the UNION

Wyoming Nickname - Equality State

EXCHANGE STUDENT

47 - FAMILY SCHEDULES

I was worried that I would have a lot of spare time during my exchange year. I thought that arriving just before the school year (knowing so little about what I was doing) would seriously limit my ability to be involved in cool after school activities. I couldn't have been more wrong, and I was busy from my first day to my last. Apparently I should have worried more about how I was going to do everything I wanted to do and how I was going to get to where I needed to go. Most sports, clubs and organizations practice or meet after school and many of them even get together on the weekends. Talk to your host parents about transportation and their schedules before you sign up. They will do everything they can to support you, but most of the time everybody has to work together to make the schedules work. For example, there were occasions that I had to wait at school longer for my host Dad to get home from work or I would have to wait until my host brother was done with his activity so I could hitch a ride home. If you are willing to work out crazy schedules with your host family, then you will be able to participate in a lot of after school activities.

TIPS...

- Discuss your schedule with your family early and often.
- Be flexible and be prepared to work around schedules of others in your host family.
- Work out rides on your own with friends who may already have their driver's license.
- Help is working out ride-shares with other kids in which your host parent may drive one day and a friend's parents on another day.

HOST PARENT

48 - HOME AWAY FROM HOME

Let's be honest, you are going to be nervous before you leave on this grand adventure and whether you admit it or not, one of your major concerns is going to be dealing with missing your family and your home. We found the best way to handle this problem is to make your new bedroom a home away from home. Bring just enough things from your own bedroom to make yourself feel like you still have a little slice of home with you in America. Bring photos of your family and your friends, and bring several meaningful items like your favorite stuffed animal or sports poster. If your host parents agree, you can even move your bedroom furniture around to locations more like your set-up at home. You will soon find out that you have limited room in the couple of suitcases you will bring to America, but it is important to bring a few things that remind you of home just in case a little homesickness creeps up on you during your time away.

DID YOU KNOW?

Approximately 29,491 high school students came to study in America during the 2010-2011 school year. The top 5 countries sending students were Germany (7,953), China (2,292), Brazil (1,983), South Korea (1,742) and Thailand (1,275). (30)

AMERICAN SLANG

My host family gave me a "nifty" looking bedroom.
(Nifty can be defined as nice, cool or fun)

STATE of the UNION

Pennsylvania State Capital - Harrisburg

EXCHANGE STUDENT

48 - HOME AWAY FROM HOME

What is home away from home you ask? Picture this in your mind; you come home from school, toss your backpack on the floor, lay your jacket over the kitchen chair, grab a snack and spread out on the living room floor to finish some school work. It is when you feel comfortable with your family, your school and your surroundings, which is what I define as HOME. Now, maybe hanging your jacket on a chair or tossing your backpack on the floor is not the best way to help keep the house clean, but it is definitely a sign that you feel like you have arrived home, and that you have successfully become a member of the family. Your exchange family is required to provide you with a house and a bedroom and this I can guarantee, but nowhere is it written that they need to make you feel like you are at home. If you and your host family work together in fostering a relationship and you follow many of the ideas presented in this book then you likely will have made a home away from home that will be available for the rest of your life.

TIPS...

- Set-up your bedroom like home.
- Hang up photos of family and friends.
- Place several knickknacks (small personal items) from your home bedroom in your exchange bedroom.
- Bring a small pillow that smells like home.
- Bring your own personal items such as your hairbrush or cologne/perfume.
- Carry reminders of home in your wallet or purse.
- If you have a pet at home, don't forget to bring special photos of them to put on your bed stand.

HOST PARENT

49 - ILLNESS and INJURY

Hopefully you will not get sick while you are away from home, but it is most likely that you are not going to escape without at least catching a cold, getting a sinus infection or scraping your knee. Like your own parents, your host parents are going to have experienced just about every sickness with their own children so they will be prepared to help you feel better. Your exchange program is going to require that you obtain special health insurance for your trip which will be necessary if your illness requires that you see a Doctor during your time in America. Your host family will also have many types of over-the-counter medications available to get you through these rough times. Don't forget to bring special medications that you may currently be using. If you have special medical conditions that your host parents need to know about, it might be a good idea to let them know in advance so they can be prepared to assist you if needed.

DID YOU KNOW?

Twenty-two million school days are lost annually in the United States due to the common cold. It is most likely that you will catch a cold during your stay in America. (31)

AMERICAN SLANG

I fell off my bike and now I have a small "boo-boo" on my elbow. (This is a small cut, scrape or injury.)

STATE of the UNION

Oregon Nickname - Beaver State

EXCHANGE STUDENT

49 - ILLNESS and INJURY

Thankfully, my illnesses were nothing more than a nasty cold in the middle of the winter and my toe turning various shades of purple after I dropped a ridiculously large shampoo bottle on it in the shower (I'm still not sure why Americans need a gallon of shampoo, so watch out toes). As an exchange student you have to purchase special health insurance before you leave and you will be provided an insurance card that you must keep with you at all times in case of illness or emergency. It is a good idea to give your host parents a copy of this card so that you always have a back-up copy if needed. One thing that is probably new to you is that many schools have their own nurse or medical professional for students that become ill during school or injured during after school sports activities. Hopefully your illness and injuries amount to nothing more than a shampoo accident and not the Swine Flu, like everybody was worried about during my stay.

TIPS...

Here are some tips to help prevent you from catching the nasty common cold:

- Because cold germs on your hands can easily enter through your eyes and nose, keep your hands away from those areas of your body.
- If possible, avoid being close to people with colds.
- If you have a cold, avoid being close to people.
- If you sneeze or cough, cover your nose and mouth, and sneeze or cough into your elbow rather than your hand. (32)

HOST PARENT

50 - PERSONAL HYGIENE

We know that you probably passed right by these two pages the first time you skimmed through the book. That's alright, we understand it is the least interesting topic in the book, but it deserves at least a little bit of attention. Americans, like many other cultures, are obsessed with personal cleanliness. Unless you are under twelve years old, you will be showering every day and most people are offended if they notice you have body odor (otherwise called B.O.). Oral hygiene (teeth cleaning and dental work) is important to Americans and most people spend a fair amount of time and money on hair and skin care. American high school kids are no different and may actually be a little more concerned about personal hygiene. So don't forget to always wear clean underwear and don't forget to wash behind your ears.

DID YOU KNOW?

Personal hygiene is associated very closely to the transmission of disease. The best way to prevent sickness is to wash your hands frequently with disinfecting soap and hot water.

AMERICAN SLANG

I can't take a shower because my host brother is taking too long in the "john". (Other words for bathroom are "john, head, restroom or toilet".)

STATE of the UNION

Vermont State Capital - Montpelier

EXCHANGE STUDENT

50 - PERSONAL HYGIENE

In your American home you will usually find one large family bathroom (also called a restroom in America) or more likely a bathroom for your parents and a bathroom for the kids. If you are lucky, you may find yourself having your own bathroom, but I would not count on that happening. Most likely you will be sharing a bathroom with either your siblings or your whole host family. If you end up sharing, there is one important task that will need to be completed right away: discussing a shower schedule. It doesn't have to be a perfect schedule with exact times, but you should decide who is going to get the bathroom in the evening and who will get it in the morning. Finally, one aspect of hygiene that was a lot of fun...yes, I said a lot of fun. Getting prepared before each school dance is as much fun as the dance itself, especially since you will be doing it with your best friends or your host siblings. You might even get your hair done which can take a long time and like me, you may find yourself painfully sitting under a hair dryer for two hours while your head feels like it is on fire! Was it worth it you ask? You may be familiar with the German saying: "Wer schön sein will, muss leiden" (or, "to look good you must suffer").

TIPS...

- Don't worry about forgetting miscellaneous items because you can find any hygiene need in America at the "corner drug store".
- Check with you host family before you leave so you do not bring something they already have (such as curling iron) that you might be able to borrow.

Dominique and her exchange siblings

Host pet Sampson

Having fun in winter

CHAPTER 3

SCHOOL STUFF

HOST PARENT

51 - THE SCHOOL DAY

School days may be a little different depending on where you live in this vast country, but there are many things that are standard. School districts have a limited number of busses and therefore they are also used for elementary and middle school kids (Kindergarten through eighth grade). To let the younger children sleep longer, high school students typically use the busses first and therefore they begin the school day earlier (usually sometime between 7:00 a.m. and 8:00 a.m.). The good news to this early start time is that you will also have an early dismissal time (typically sometime between 2:00 p.m. and 3:00 p.m.). One item that you may find different than in your own country is that once your American school day has been determined it will not likely change for the entire year. Sure, your classes may change and your lunch period may change, but your start time and end time will probably be the same between September and June. You will find that having a consistent school day is necessary so you can fit in all your after school activities. Isn't that right Dominique?

DID YOU KNOW?

Did you know that public schools are free to all U.S. Citizens? Many people elect to pay for private (typically religious based) schools because they think a better education is provided.

AMERICAN SLANG

Let me give you the "skinny" on a typical American school day. (This means to get information or an explanation about something.)

EXCHANGE STUDENT

51 - THE SCHOOL DAY

That's right Scott, it didn't take long for me to get used to the American school day. Each semester I got up at the same time, went to the same six classes and I had the same lunch period. Maybe this sounds boring, but this routine was necessary for me to keep my crazy American life in order. Before my first hour began I would find my friends and we would talk about our schedule for the day and often we would make plans for after school or for the weekend. Like in your own country, you will study different subjects throughout the day, but in America you will actually go to a different room and have a different teacher for each subject. Your class time is referred to as a "period" and lasts for about 45 to 50 minutes with 5 or 10 minutes to change rooms and visit your locker. Your after school activities will be anything but boring and you will quickly see that you can't fit everything into your day. Soccer, band, cheerleading or play practice can eat up 2 or 3 hours of time every day after school. Combine your school day with your after school activities and then add in your family life, chores and homework and well...it's time for bed so you can do it all over again.

TIPS...

- Schedule your locker visits during times when you are near your locker.
- Take time before school or during lunch to plan for rides and after school/weekend activities with your friends.
- Don't schedule too many activities or you may get behind with your school work.

STATE of the UNION

Florida State Capital - Tallahassee

HOST PARENT

52 - SCHOOL STRUCTURE

Most American schools are grouped together in districts. These districts are defined differently depending on where you live in the United States. Typically they are grouped together by county or city. Most school districts have elementary schools (kindergarten through fourth grade) spread out through the neighborhoods so many young children can actually walk to school and are familiar with their surroundings. Several larger middle schools/junior high schools (grades five through eight) are located within the district for the pre-teenage students. Finally, a school district will have at least one large high school (grades nine through twelve) that will be on a very large plot of land with the school building and associated facilities for extracurricular activities. American school districts are set up like small governments and they have an administrative staff that runs the day-to-day activities, while a publically elected "board of education" watches over the district and makes formal policy and business decisions.

DID YOU KNOW?

Did you know American High Schools are categorized by their size? During State or National competitions for various events, high schools usually complete against other high schools within their size classification. For example, in Michigan, the largest are usually AAA and the smallest are typically D (with AA, A, B, and C in between).

AMERICAN SLANG

The state football championship is "up for grabs". (This means it is anybody's to win.)

STATE of the UNION

Maine Nickname - Pine Tree State

EXCHANGE STUDENT

52 - SCHOOL STRUCTURE

American high schools are very organized places and most of them are like miniature cities. The Main Office is where you will find the school administrators, like the Principal or Assistant Principals, who are in charge of the school. This is the place where you will register for school, sign in or out of school, call home if needed or even leave a message in a teacher's mail box. At the Counseling Office you will find your assigned Counselor who will help you pick classes, assist you with changing classes if one does not work out or who will even assist if you are having difficulties with a student or a teacher. You will eat lunch in the school cafeteria where you will find a friendly staff to serve you. Does your high school at home have a store? Your American high school will have a student run store where you can buy anything from a t-shirt (with your mascot) to school supplies or cookies and candy. The librarian will assist you in locating a book or finding information on a computer. I found help from students and staff no matter where I went or what I was doing, so relax because your American school staff will take care of everything.

FACTS...

Many high schools are huge and they typically have more than just the school building. You will usually find the following structures associated with your school building:

- Athletic Facilities including a football stadium, gymnasium & track as well as baseball, softball and soccer Fields. Tennis courts and a large pool (natatorium) will also be at your school.
- Activity Facilities including band rooms, auditorium and large media center (library) and school store.

HOST PARENT

53 - SCHOOL RULES

There have been two events in the recent past that have significantly changed attitudes and rules at school buildings throughout America. In 1999 two students at Columbine High School in Colorado planned and carried out the worst U.S. high school massacre ever. They killed twelve students and one teacher and injured twenty-one others before they shot themselves. Most of the world is familiar with the second event that has changed many rules in the United States. The 2001 terrorist attack on the World Trade Center in New York City has made everybody look at security issues in all public buildings, including schools. I'm sure nobody has to tell you that weapons are not allowed at school, but you should know that making threats or even joking about issues related to these topics are treated very seriously. Schools are shut down immediately if a student makes a physical threat to another or even if somebody jokes about a bomb or a weapon. Follow these rules without question or you will find yourself expelled from school and in serious trouble with the police.

DID YOU KNOW?

Did you know that every American high school student is assigned a counselor (including exchange students)? Your counselor will assist you with any concerns or questions you have with your schedule or any personal issues, including information you may want to know about school rules.

AMERICAN SLANG

Make sure you are "all ears" when the rules are explained.

(If you are all ears you are ready to listen closely.)

STATE of the UNION

Alabama State Capital - Montgomery

EXCHANGE STUDENT

53 - SCHOOL RULES

Rule #1: Listen to the rules. Rule #2: Follow all the rules. Rule #3: If you break the rules make sure you don't get caught. Although I had heard rumors about American high schools having a lot of rules, I was a little surprised that there were so many. On the first day of school everybody was provided a rule booklet and we reviewed these rules for several days (or at least it seemed like several days). This small page does not provide nearly enough room to detail all of rules, but here are a few school rules that will give you a little idea of what I mean. You have to be on time to class or you will be marked tardy. If you are very late to class then you will be marked as absent. You cannot take your backpack, food or drink into your classrooms. Do not even think about using the restroom or leaving your classroom for any reason without having a "hall pass". Also, let's not forget about all the rules of your sports team or your club! What happens if you break the rules you ask? Breaking rules can result in any number of unpleasant things that could include picking up trash, sweeping floors or classroom detention. Most of these rules are easy to follow, but in case you don't like following rules then you should be prepared to spend a little extra time in school after your last class.

TIPS...

- *Detention* - Minor school violations require you to stay after school with a teacher and do homework.
- *Suspension* - If you break a more serious rule you might be sent home for several days.
- *Expulsion* - Doing something seriously wrong may get you kicked out of school permanently.

HOST PARENT

54 - TOP OF THE CLASS

When writing your exchange student profile for your exchange agency you should know that almost every other student completing the same forms is between fifteen and eighteen years old, which places them in the 10th, 11th or 12th grade. What you might not know is that (no matter where you come from) you are probably not familiar with the freshman, sophomore, junior and senior ranking system utilized in America. It does not matter what year of school you are in at your real home, you will now be placed into one of these "classes". You may be placed in the class that represents your age or you may be placed in the senior class so you can get the experience full experience of the "final year" in an American high school. This was great for our exchange student (and for any foreign exchange student) since she was able to experience many more fun activities as a senior such as prom, senior week and other exclusive activities reserved for these "upper classmen".

DID YOU KNOW?

That elderly people in the United States are referred to as Senior Citizens and that that students in their last (12th) year of high school are also called seniors. According to the English dictionary, a senior *"is a person older than another"*. (33)

AMERICAN SLANG

I "aced" my biology test today. (Getting an A or acing the test means you got the best/top mark available.)

EXCHANGE STUDENT

54 - TOP OF THE CLASS

There are four grades in the American high school which are divided into two groups: freshmen and sophomores who are called lower classmen and the juniors and seniors who are called the upper classmen. Fortunately you are most likely old enough to be an upper classman. This is important because lower classmen have it more difficult since they are younger and are often given a hard time by the upper classmen. Everybody identifies themselves by the grade they are in and many fun activities and contests take place between the grades. All this competition and teasing each other is always in good fun and in the end loyalty to your high school is much more important than loyalty to your grade.

TIPS...

- Your locker locations are usually better as you work your way up the "class" ladder.
- Juniors and seniors (if their schedule allows) will usually get the best lunch time.
- The first several days at school can be daunting and it may be necessary for an upper classman to help you with your locker combination or assist in finding your classroom.

Most seniors will agree that the best thing about their last year is being at the top of the class and playing tricks with the lower classmen...have fun.

STATE of the UNION

Nevada Nickname - Silver State

HOST PARENT

55 - GRADES and ATTENDANCE

My exchange daughter took the subject of grades and left me with the completely boring topic of attendance. Believe it or not, your host parents are concerned about these topics and are certainly involved with your attendance requirements. Your American school year is divided into two semesters: fall/winter and winter/spring. During each semester you are allowed a specific number of excused absences (in our high school it is 10) or rather a certain number of days that you can miss without getting into trouble. If you are going to miss a school day, your host parents will be required to contact the school and inform them about your absence and provide them with a reason. Almost any reason to miss school is acceptable including the most popular reason; a family vacation. Just remember to find out what the school absence rules are and never forget to have one of your host parents call when you won't be there, including your sick days. Most importantly, don't miss school without telling your host parents because the school will call them and you may find yourself in after school detention.

DID YOU KNOW?

Did you know that a person that gets an "A" in every class through high school is called a Valedictorian? This is a student with a 4.0 GPA since A's are worth 4 points, B's are worth 3 points, C's are worth 2 points, D's are worth 1 point and E's/F's are worth 0.

AMERICAN SLANG

The test was a "breeze"! (The test was easy and not difficult at all.)

STATE of the UNION

Ohio State Capital - Columbus

EXCHANGE STUDENT

55 - GRADES and ATTENDANCE

A, B, C, D, E, and F. This may look like the first six letters of the alphabet but did you know it is also the American grading system? An "A" is the best and equals a "1" in my country while an "F" is the worst and equals the "6" that you never want to show your parents (in either country). Remember, "F" means "fail" and in your American high school you will not get credit for this class and you will have to take it again the next school year. What are credits you ask? American high schools require that each student has a certain amount of credits in order to graduate. Of those credits, they are required to have a specific amount of English, math, social studies, science and foreign language credits. These credits don't really matter to you since you are an exchange student, but the grades you receive do matter. You will receive a report card at the end of each semester at which time the Americans make it confusing by assigning a number value to each grade and then dividing that number by your number of classes to give you a "grade point average" (GPA). Make your host parents proud and come home with a 4.0 GPA.

TIPS...

- Participation is always an important part of your class grades in America.
- Most classes have many quizzes (small tests) that take place every week. Each quiz is worth points.
- Semester ending tests are called "Finals" and typically make up a large portion of your grade (points).
- If you miss school it is your responsibility to make up your work, take a missed test and turn in missing work.

HOST PARENT

56 - LOCKERS and BACKPACKS

I'll pass on backpacks, we didn't even know what they were in 1980, but lockers have been around in American high schools as long as there have been American high schools. Lockers are the one place in high school that you can call your own and the time you spend there between classes is often the most fun part of the school day. You can talk to friends, make plans or just hang out, even if it is for only five minutes. (It is possible since you are an exchange student you may get a locker with the seniors, but don't count on it unless you actually are a senior). Now, keep in mind that most of your American classmates have been using lockers for many years and don't be afraid to ask for help in working the combination lock on your locker (yes, your locker must remain closed and locked while you are not using it). It is almost a real profession trying to get these things to work properly.

DID YOU KNOW?

An exchange student at our school figured out that during the course of the year you will spend almost 4 hours opening your locker. This is how he figured it:

175 school days x 8 times per day x 10 seconds to get your locker open = 14,000 seconds which = 233 minutes which = 3.8 hours—WOW!!

AMERICAN SLANG

My locker is "jam packed" with books and supplies!

(This is another way of saying something is completely full.)

STATE of the UNION

Texas Nickname - Lone Star State

EXCHANGE STUDENT

56 - LOCKERS and BACKPACKS

In my home country we are required to carry our books, folders and supplies around with us in our backpack. In America, the books are thicker and heavier and you are required to change classrooms every hour (don't worry; you won't have more homework just because the books are bigger). On your first day at school you will be provided a locker that will be yours for the entire year. This locker is essential for the storage of all your books, supplies, coats, boots, and gym bag and after school needs. You will be so busy at school that sometimes it may feel like you are actually living out of your locker. Most schools give you 5 to 10 minutes between classes to get to your locker and to your next classroom. You may even have a few minutes left to have a quick conversation with your best friend. Since you will most likely be an upper classman you will probably get a great locker location and not be stuck in a far away spot with all the freshmen. Have you ever seen those American TV shows where the bully's lock a kid in his own locker? Don't worry; the lockers I've seen in America are hardly big enough to fit one leg!

TIPS...

- If you are having trouble getting to your locker for a certain class you may be able to share a closer locker with a friend.
- Never leave expensive things in your locker, like a calculator, as it may get stolen.
- You are allowed to decorate the inside of your locker with posters, mirrors and other personal items.

HOST PARENT

57 - CLUBS

If you can't find something to keep you busy in an American high school, then you are a person with absolutely no interests. There are clubs for this interest, clubs for that interest and there are even clubs for your interest; I promise. (If your school does not have a club that you are interested in joining, then feel free to start a new club.) In our high school you can join the band, orchestra, jazz band, drum line, color guard (flags & rifles in band), Key Club (community service), S.A.D.D. (students against destructive decisions), Quiz Bowl (trivia club), Act2 (theatre), Cancer Awareness Club, Finance Club, Yearbook Staff, News Staff, P.P.I. (Positive Peer Influence), B.P.A. (Business Professionals of America), Bible Study and Corners Club (diversity club). There is also the National Honor Society (for students with great grades) and student government (Class President, Vice President, etc.). These are just the clubs I can think of without getting a complete list from the school and I am beginning to run out of room on the page. Now I think you are beginning to see what I mean when I say that there IS something for you in your new American high school. Don't be afraid to give one a try.

DID YOU KNOW?

Did you know that you don't have to be in a sports club to compete? Many of these other clubs compete against each other on State and National levels. Examples are the bands, choirs and the B.P.A. or the Quiz Bowl.

AMERICAN SLANG

That play was really "wicked"! (This is really cool.)

STATE of the UNION

Illinois State Capital - Springfield

EXCHANGE STUDENT

57 - CLUBS

Without a doubt there are more sports clubs (or teams) than anything else in a typical American high school, but you don't have to be the athletic type to be in a club. There are so many other kinds of clubs that you are sure to find something of interest. I joined the theatre club only because it sounded interesting and I had heard people talk about how much fun it is. When I joined, they were preparing for the annual "musical" and auditions were scheduled. I signed up to work as a stage hand or to do a different off-stage task such as lighting or sound, but that quickly changed. As I met more people and they found out I was an exchange student, they quickly took an interest in my involvement. They talked me into trying out for a role in the musical and I ended up being selected for the chorus (dancers & singers). The theatre club was everything and more that I had hoped it would be. People you meet in your club will become your best friends and you will work together for a common goal that will be both educational and thrilling. Alright, so I might not be the next Angelina Jolie, but who cares because I had the best time of my life.

FACTS...

- Some clubs meet monthly while others meet every day.
- There may be some costs to join certain clubs or to participate in certain activities, but most are free.
- Many schools require a payment to join a sports club. This recent trend has been labeled "pay to play" and is used to cover sports equipment and upkeep costs.

HOST PARENT

58 - WHAT TO WEAR

School uniforms are only required if you are attending a private (parochial) high school in America. You will most likely be attending a public high school where uniforms are not required, but certain minimal rules will be enforced. Rules are slightly different at each school. My exchange daughter has done a nice job explaining typical rules you can expect at your high school. As a parent I am always worried about proper clothing for the outside weather conditions. Often times, kids will not wear proper clothing because they just don't look cool. It is not uncommon to see somebody standing in the rain without a coat or walking in a winter storm wearing only a spring jacket. I have also observed exchange students from hot climates coming to America unprepared for the weather conditions in their American city. Essentials like boots, gloves and hats will probably be needed at some time. If you don't have room to pack yours, than plan on shopping soon after your arrive. Remember that you can always borrow from your host family and your new best friends.

DID YOU KNOW?

Did you know you will be arriving in America just in time for all of the "back to school" sales in the clothing stores? Some favorite American stores for high school kids are Hollister, American Eagle, Abercrombie & Fitch, Aeropostale and Old Navy.

AMERICAN SLANG

My girlfriends and I got "all dolled up" for the dance.
(Dressing up, make-up on and hair done or just looking great.)

STATE of the UNION

Kansas Nickname - Sunflower State

EXCHANGE STUDENT

58 - WHAT TO WEAR

As you have probably heard many times, Americans can be very conservative people. I am not sure that has anything to do with the school dress codes, but it is not as bad as you might think. These rules may seem very strict, but don't forget they are school rules and you typically can wear whatever you want at home. At school you are not allowed to wear hats, coats or shirts with references to drugs, alcohol, violence, etc. Your shoulders have to be covered, which means that if you want to wear a tank top you have to wear a sweater over it. You probably know from your home country that, especially for girls, skirts and shorts can't be too short. At my American school, we had the "finger-tip-rule". There's an easy way to check if your shorts or skirt are too short to wear to school: stand up straight, put your hands down along your body and the point where your finger-tips touch your leg is how long your shorts or skirt must be. These are just a few examples of dress rules. Your school's rules may be slightly different. Take the rules seriously because your school will check and I have had friends who were actually sent home to change their clothes.

TIPS...

- Check the climate in your American city so you can properly prepare for the weather.
- Don't over-pack clothing since you will probably be buying many things while you are in America.
- You may borrow clothing from your host siblings if you are the same size (just like you may do at home now).
- Figure out your American "sizes" so you can easily find your favorite outfit at the mall.

HOST PARENT

59 - FOOTBALL

I was not sure if our exchange student would like football, but I did know that she was going to have to deal with it one way or another. No matter what country you come from, you will most likely understand football to be soccer. American football has become our national past time and it is so interwoven into our culture that we forget how uniquely American it is. We have high school football, college football, professional football, touch football, arena football and even powder-puff (girl) football—most of which have not been experienced by students outside of North America. It is impossible for students to not attend high school games, but we also took our student to a college game so she could get the collegiate experience. Many foreign students enroll in American Universities and this was a great chance to check one out. I tried to explain the rules, but I eventually gave up after realizing how silly the game actually is.

DID YOU KNOW?

It is estimated that over 90 million people watch the Super Bowl every year. In 2011, it was the highest watched TV show ever. The Super Bowl is the championship game for professional American Football.

AMERICAN SLANG

Why do football players think they are such "big shots"?

(Big shots think they are the best or better than everybody else.)

STATE of the UNION

Rhode Island State Capital - Providence

EXCHANGE STUDENT

59 - FOOTBALL

Football? Before I left my country I had heard a lot of people speak about how much Americans love this sport. I quickly found out that Football and America go together like peanut butter and jelly. (Oh, you don't know about that one either?). Football, or should I say "American Football" is a weird game where a bunch of guys (usually) chase each other around trying to tackle the guy who has a ball that is not even shaped like a ball. In fact, this football, which is not football to the rest of the world, usually does not come into contact with their feet...oh, so confusing. American school years begin in September so it will only take a few days before most exchange students attend their first high school football game. I never really did figure out the rules but I quickly found out it didn't matter because the game was like a social event for students, parents and people in the community. Because of these football games I was able to hang out with friends and it was a place where I could meet many new people of all ages. If you are wondering, yes I have my own football and I dare you to try and tackle me.

FACTS...
Touchdowns = 7 points
Field Goals = 3 points
Four Quarters = 1 game

Don't miss the marching bands that always play at "half time" -rain or shine.

HOST PARENT

60 - CHEERLEADING

If you have watched any American high school movie, then you've probably seen cheerleaders. Just as the name implies, they are people (usually students) who lead cheers for their sports team. Although cheerleading began at the college level and is comprised of young men and women, you will typically only find cheerleading teams of girls at your exchange high school. Although you may see cheerleaders at a basketball game or a wrestling match, you will not miss them on Friday night at the football game wearing a sweater and skirt with the school colors. Cheerleading is so popular that it is a sport in itself and cheerleading teams from all over the country complete against each other. In recent years most high schools have also organized a pom-pom squad that are really "dance" teams performing at football games and competitions. "Let's go red. Let's go white, let's go red, let's go white, fight, fight, fight!!"

DID YOU KNOW?

The Universal Cheerleading Association holds a national high school cheerleading competition every year. This is so popular that you can actually watch the competition on television in America or maybe in your home country.

STATE of the UNION

Hawaii Nickname - Aloha State

EXCHANGE STUDENT

60 - CHEERLEADING

What is cheerleading? I had never heard of such a thing and we certainly don't have any cheerleaders at my home school. Think of gymnastics with a group of girls wearing matching skirts and sweaters while all yelling a "cheer" that rhymes and motivates the crowd at a sporting event (usually football or basketball). They dance, jump, flip, tumble and make different formations all while yelling out their cheers. Just as you might have seen in the movies, many of these girls are pretty and popular which often creates a stereotype that they are mean and arrogant. I found that they are just like everybody else and have enjoyed being friends with several cheerleaders. "Let's go Pirates!"

FACTS...

- The first college to have cheerleading was The University of Minnesota.
- The Dallas Cowboy (professional football) Cheerleaders are the most famous cheerleaders in America.
- Pom Pom squads (also at most American High Schools) are not cheerleaders, but they are more like a dance team that have similar uniforms.

AMERICAN SLANG

You have to be "perky" to be a good cheerleader. (To be perky is to be cheerful, excited and happy.)

HOST PARENT

61 - MARCHING BAND

I cannot lie: I was a band geek in high school and I'm proud to say that I enjoyed every moment of it! I'm sure that you know little more about marching bands than what you may have seen in the movies or on television. To be honest, band camp is not like what you learned in the movie *"American Pie"*. For many students, the marching band half-time show at the football games may be more exciting than the game itself. Just because you have probably never participated in a marching band does not mean that you do not play an instrument or that you are not musically inclined. Your exchange high school has many other musical options such as concert band, jazz band, vocal music or orchestra. You may speak a different language at home, but remember that music is an international language that is the same for all of us.

DID YOU KNOW?

The Sousaphone was named after John Phillip Sousa and is a tuba that wraps around a person's body making it easier to march with and easier to hear.

AMERICAN SLANG

You don't have to be a "nerd" to be in the band. (Nerds are smart, intellectual and usually stereotyped as unattractive. This is not really true.)

STATE of the UNION

Arizona State Capital - Phoenix

EXCHANGE STUDENT

61 - MARCHING BAND

Marching band and bands of all kinds are very popular in American high schools. Marching band is like a regular band on steroids. It is a way for music students to have fun playing their instruments while participating in many school spirit activities. These activities include half-time shows at football games, marching in parades, competing against other bands and playing outdoor concerts. The main purpose of a marching band is to march on the football field while making various formations and playing music to a theme. Marching band takes a lot of time and the students spend many hours practicing these shows. As an exchange student it was fun watching all the kids marching in the same uniform and trying to find my friends when they all look the same. Band students are crazy, smart and fun...hang out with them and you'll see what I mean.

FACTS...

- The "color guard" is a section in the marching band that tosses flags and rifles as part of the show.
- Marching bands actually compete against each other and it is so popular that you can join "corps" that play and compete all summer long.
- Most high schools have "pep bands," smaller versions of marching bands that play at basketball games or other indoor sporting events.

HOST PARENT

62 - HOMECOMING and PROM

Sure, almost every teenager from every country has attended some type of sporting event and some type of dance, but probably not an entire week of activities built around one high school football game. (For that matter, activities begin several weeks before the big game.) This is an experience not to be missed by any exchange student. Think back to all the fun homecoming activities you may have participated in: building a float, marching in the parade, attending pep rallies, and, of course, the big football game followed by the homecoming dance. Date or no date, your exchange student WILL want to attend one of these dances, but they will need help with all the usual items such as a shirt and tie, dress and flowers. This is absolutely one of the best times of an American school year and one that will leave an impression on your student for life...don't let them miss out.

DID YOU KNOW?

Many American schools have a "Sadie Hawkins" dance. Named after an old comic strip character, this dance requires the girl to ask the boy to the dance.

AMERICAN SLANG

Everybody was "grinding" on the dance floor. (This is a dance craze where couples dance too close together.)

STATE of the UNION

Oklahoma Nickname - Sooner State

EXCHANGE STUDENT

62 - HOMECOMING and PROM

Wow...fun, fun, fun and more fun. Homecoming is a big part of the American school year. Homecoming is many things: the celebration of the new school year, the end of the football season and the "coming home" of past students. Homecoming week or sometimes called spirit week, includes such things as pep assemblies, class floats, parade, football game and, of course, the homecoming dance. As an exchange student you can participate in all these events, including my favorite—marching in the parade with our volleyball team and tossing candy to the children watching the parade. Prom is similar to homecoming except it is a celebration typically for seniors who are completing their last year of high school. Both events include a formal dance where the boys dress in suits and the girls in dresses. School dances in America are a lot of fun and I am very happy that I had a chance to attend all of them.

TIPS...

- Girls typically buy boys boutonnieres to be pinned to their lapels.
- Boys typically buy girls corsages that are worn on their wrist or shoulder.

FACTS...

- Prom is short for Promenade and is a formal dance typically held near the end of the school year.
- No matter their age, past graduates come back to play in the band during the homecoming football game.

HOST PARENT

63 - SCHOOL BUS

What can I tell you about a school bus that you haven't already experienced while waiting for a city bus? Waiting in the cold, standing in the rain, snow in your boots, bus running late, uncomfortable seats, and don't forget the infamous mean school bus driver. There may be nothing new to tell you about American school busses other than they are truly unique. Most exchange students walk, ride their bikes, ride a city bus or use some other type of public transportation to get to school in their home country. The idea of riding the classic "Blue Bird" yellow colored school bus may bring back bad memories for your host parents, but it will be a classic American experience for you. In a practical matter, this may be your main source of transportation to and from your American school and hopefully it will not be a new source of bad dreams.

DID YOU KNOW?

That in accordance with U.S. law, school busses are required to be yellow. This shade of yellow is a color so distinct that it is now known as "school bus yellow".

AMERICAN SLANG

After your trip to America you are never going to want to take a "spin" in a school bus again. (This is to drive or take a ride.)

STATE of the UNION

West Virginia State Capital - Charleston

EXCHANGE STUDENT

63 - SCHOOL BUS

You can't miss them; they are everywhere...bright yellow school busses. If you were not lucky enough to get a host family with high school age siblings that drive to school, then you will be relying on one of these school busses. It takes longer, they have hard seats, they are cold in the winter and hot in the summer, but they are free and they are dependable. The school busses are owned by the school system and they pick you up and drop you off right in your neighborhood. You will ride the bus with your siblings and friends and you will even meet new friends on the ride that seems to take much too long. If you get permission you can even take your friend's school bus to their home for after school fun. Even if you have an alternate way to get to school make sure you take the school bus once in a while just so you can experience the "big yellow bird".

FACTS...

- School busses are typically owned by the school or school district.
- School busses are smaller and less comfortable than city busses.
- School start times are staggered since there are usually not enough busses to get everybody to school at the same time.

HOST PARENT

64 - SCHOOL LUNCH

Even though I am way past my high school years, lunch is still my favorite meal of the day. It is still the time I am able to take a break and talk about fun things not related to school (oops, I mean work). Just as you will be learning about our American culture, we have just as much fun learning about yours. Our student said her lunch was like our dinner and her dinner was like our lunch and she ate lunch earlier and dinner later and...well I think you get the picture. One thing was common between us—we were able to share good food and we had a lot of fun doing it no matter where or what time. Lunch at school is fun too. Be sure you experience both a "bag" lunch from your exchange home and a school bought lunch. I am sure school lunches are much better than they were back in 19—. (Does it really matter when I finished high school?)

DID YOU KNOW?

The National School Lunch Program became a law in 1946 under President Harry Truman and was established to provide a low cost or free lunch to school children. (34)

AMERICAN SLANG

The school lunch tasted "crappy" today! (Everybody knows that this is a bad or disgusting thing.)

STATE of the UNION

Minnesota Nickname - North Star State

EXCHANGE STUDENT

64 - SCHOOL LUNCH

No doubt about it, lunch is the best part of the school day. It is the one time you are not sitting in class listening to a lecture or completing an assignment, but rather a time to re-fuel while hanging out with your friends and making after-school or weekend plans. Lunch is so much different than at my home school where we just hang out in a hallway or a classroom and have a light snack. In America you will likely be assigned a specific lunch period (A, B, C, or more) and eat in a cafeteria. Your lunch is more like a meal and you will either bring a "packed" lunch or you can purchase a hot lunch like pizza, chicken strips or a salad. The cafeteria is filled with lunch tables and you will find yourself meeting up with your good friends and often it is the best place to meet new friends. At the beginning of each semester, most kids find a lunch table with friends and they usually sit together every day at the same table. Lunch was my favorite class. What? It's not a class?

FACTS...

- The average school purchased lunch costs about $3.00 U.S. dollars.
- Most lunch periods are around 30 minutes.
- Most schools have two or three lunch periods (times) that you may be assigned.
- Many schools do not allow students to leave the building for lunch. Your school will be either designated a "closed campus" or an "open campus".

HOST PARENT

65 - SOCCER

In the past twenty years, soccer (European football) has become a very popular sport to play, but with all the efforts to create a passion for the game, Americans still do not seem to care for the sport beyond high school. It seems that just about everybody born before 1985 has little or no interest, but with every passing year it is changing. You will find very little soccer on television and, although there is a professional league in the United States, you may find that you are not living close enough to attend a live game. If you happen to be studying here during a World Cup, you will finally see some soccer as many Americans are now starting to take interest as the American team is beginning to show some talent. If you are a player, well, that is something entirely different because there are plenty of places to play—school teams, community/amateur teams or pick-up games with your friends. Almost all schools have multiple soccer teams and you will find the talent level very competitive. If soccer is your thing, then don't forget to pack your ball, spikes and shin guards and get ready to shine.

DID YOU KNOW?

The most famous soccer player in America is a woman—Mia Hamm. She has won the FIFA Player of the Year twice and was on the 2004 U.S. gold medal team.

STATE of the UNION

New York State Capital - Albany

EXCHANGE STUDENT

65 - SOCCER

Don't even think about calling soccer football. American's might forgive you for being a soccer fan, but they will not forgive you for calling it football. In America there is only one game called football and it does not involve a round ball. If you are from a country that loves soccer (which is just about everywhere outside of America) and you love to play the game, then you will get plenty of opportunities. Soccer is popular with young Americans and you will find plenty of teams to join. Boys' soccer is typically in autumn and at my school every male exchange student (10 total) played on the school team. Although you will find several good American players, the exchange students quickly became the talk of the school in regards to their soccer talents. So you are a girl? Don't worry, girls' soccer is just as big here and you will have the same opportunity to score a point for the team.

FACTS...

- Most people in America do not know the rules of soccer.
- Most Americans born before 1970 have never played the game competitively.
- Soccer is now one of the fastest growing sports in America.

AMERICAN SLANG

I just don't understand why American's think soccer is such a "lame" sport. (This means it is bad, a poor idea or just unconvincing.)

HOST PARENT

66 - ATHLETICS

It often seems like sports are more important in American schools than reading, writing and arithmetic. Every high school has multiple sports teams for boys and girls. As an exchange student you will be allowed to join any of these teams, but be prepared to take it seriously and prepared to spend a lot of time. Practice is mandatory and there is a lot of it. Practice before school, after school and sometimes during school is common. All teams compete against other schools for league championships and then for state championships. Although school is free in the United States, most schools now charge to join sports teams in order to help pay for team costs—these programs are called "Pay to Play". If you want to excel at your sport, then you are coming to the right place.

DID YOU KNOW?
You can join any of these teams at your American High School: Baseball, Softball, Basketball, Volleyball, Football, Soccer, Swimming, Wrestling, Hockey, Tennis, Track, Cross Country, Gymnastics and Bowling.

AMERICAN SLANG
He is acting just like I expect a "jock" to act. (This is person who loves and plays many sports.)

STATE of the UNION
Connecticut Nickname - Constitution State

EXCHANGE STUDENT

66 - ATHLETICS

Here is a common sight in my American high school at 7:00 a.m. before your first class—students walking around in sweatpants, in team jerseys, in cheerleading sweaters, with bottles of water, with wet hair and wearing flip-flops. This peculiar behavior is related to all the different sports teams in high school and all the early morning (or late afternoon) team practice sessions. Sports are a big and important part of American schools and many students belong to one or more of these teams. As an exchange student you are allowed to belong to any one of these teams but be warned: you will need to try-out, you will need to be good and you will need to commit a lot of time (several hours per day). On the other hand, if you don't make the best team there is usually more than one team per sport so don't give up if you really want to participate. Athletics is one of the best ways to experience true "School Spirit" and compete against other area high schools.

FACTS...

- In recent years, many schools have been charging a fee to play sports in schools. These "Pay to Play" programs are used to assist fund the high cost of athletics in schools.
- There are so many sports available to students that most schools have an Athletic Director who is responsible for the oversight of schedules, coaches and programs.
- Participation in sports varies from school to school. If a school is very competitive in a particular sport (such as football), they may not accept an exchange student on the team. Other schools will have no problem putting an exchange student on any team.

HOST PARENT

67 - SNOW DAYS

Unfortunately, only students and teachers get snow days while the rest of the working world in America must attempt to get to work regardless of road conditions or snow accumulation. While we are risking our lives getting to work, you may just be working on your beauty sleep. Weather is unpredictable so it is likely that you will need to get up early and watch the television news to find out if your school (school district) has been cancelled...if so, crawl right back under the covers and dream about the fun you are going to have on your free day. For the rest of you exchange students lucky enough to be placed in a warm climate you may not experience a snow day, but you will experience something not often viewed in a northern winter—the sun. Sunshine or snowfall, weather will have some affect on your school year and all you have to do is make the best of it.

DID YOU KNOW?

Did you know that 10 inches of snow (25 centimeters) is equal to about 1 inch (2.5 centimeters) of liquid rain? (35)

AMERICAN SLANG

If we have another snow day tomorrow I'm just going to "veg" all day. (Veg is short for vegetable and it means somebody is lying around and doing nothing.)

STATE of the UNION

Missouri State Capital - Jefferson City

EXCHANGE STUDENT

67 - SNOW DAYS

America is a huge place and you may be wishing that you get selected by a family living in a warm location. Chances are just as likely that you will end up in a place that gets snow and in some locations...a lot of snow. Don't worry, these locations have something really cool called a "snow day". My school was cancelled if the temperature was at -10 degrees Fahrenheit (with wind chill factor) or if snow accumulated quicker than they could keep the roads clear. Why are they fun? It is just like a vacation day and you can sleep in, watch television, have your friends over (when the roads clear), watch movies and mostly relax. I was told there are some rituals you can do to help create a snow day like flushing ice cubes down the toilet or wearing your pajamas inside out. I can confirm these crazy methods did not work, but Mother Nature provided several snow days during my stay and hopefully you'll experience several yourselves.

FACTS...

Interesting facts according to the National Snow and Ice Data Center: (36)

- Practically every place in America has seen snowfall, even southern Florida has had snow flurries.
- In the early 1990's, skiers created their own terminology for snow conditions: fluffy, powder and sticky snow.
- New York State has some of the snowiest cities in America.
- Approximately 105 snowstorms affect the U.S. every year.

HOST PARENT

68 - SCHOOL SPIRIT

What is school spirit? In my opinion, it is the love you have for your school and everything associated with it. By now you are beginning to understand that the life of an American teenager is completely associated with their high school. School spirit is the way you show your loyalty to your school. It is the way you cheer for your friends, your teams and your organizations. School spirit is about making friends, acting crazy, screaming out loud, dressing funny, taunting the other team, dancing to the band and making memories for a lifetime. I still have school spirit for my high school even though I graduated over 25 years ago and you will have it even though you will only be involved for one year. School spirit is timeless and I promise you that your American high school will be in your mind and your heart for the rest of your life.

DID YOU KNOW?

Did you know American college also have mascots. These are some of the most common mascots you will find: Eagles, Tigers, Bulldogs, Panthers, Knights, Lions, Bears, Hawks, Cougars and Pioneers. (37)

AMERICAN SLANG

My host dad was a little "sappy" in this story. (A sappy person is a very sentimental person.)

STATE of the UNION

New Mexico Nickname - Land of Enchantment

EXCHANGE STUDENT

68 - SCHOOL SPIRIT

Let's get to the basics of school spirit: every American high school has a mascot and school colors. At my school, we were Pirates and our colors were red and black. To be honest, I had no idea what everybody was talking about when they said "show us your school spirit". I quickly understood that it was a feeling of loyalty and pride for your school and that there are many ways of expressing these feelings. I first experienced it during "homecoming" week at the beginning of the school year during a week appropriately called "Spirit Week". Students dressed according to daily themes like pajama day, toga day, miss-match day and school colors day (sure we looked stupid, but that was half the fun of it). Posters were hung around the school announcing various fun activities and there was even a "pep assembly" held in the gymnasium to get everybody in a school spirit mood. Speeches were made, cheerleaders performed and the band played the school "fight song" while the red and black crowd clapped along. What can I say about school spirit other than ...LETS GO PIRATES!!!!

TIPS...

- Find out your school colors before you come and pack some matching clothing.
- Don't be embarrassed to join in the fun otherwise you will miss out on the best part of high school.
- You don't have to be on a sports team to have school spirit. Go watch and cheer for your school.
- School spirit is more than a sports team. You can join a club, see a school play or compete on an academic team.

HOST PARENT

69 - FINE ARTS

Fine arts have always played an important role in American schools. Fine arts include graphic art, vocal music, instrumental music and drama. All of these art programs are offered as elective courses in American high schools and are part of the daily curriculum. You are not required to take any of these classes, but you may find something fun or interesting that is not offered in your school at home. Most instrumental and vocal music classes are also music groups that often compete against other school programs. You may even perform individually where you can be adjudicated and awarded medals based on your performance. Visual art students can also enter shows to display their work or compete against other students. Finally, drama students audition and perform in various plays, musicals and festivals that occur throughout the year. Although funding in recent years has drastically reduced the amount of these courses offered you will still find the basics in most American high schools.

DID YOU KNOW?

Art (and Craft) shows can be found in cities and towns all over America during the spring and summer months. These are called street fairs or art fairs and some even have a catchy name like "Art in the Park".

AMERICAN SLANG

I went to the school play last night and it was "the bomb" (Kids say this when something is a huge hit or if something great.)

EXCHANGE STUDENT

69 - FINE ARTS

If you are talented in music, art or theatre, then you will find plenty of opportunities to practice your skills in any American high school. In my country we have a choice of an art class or a music class, but in America I had so many choices it was hard to believe. For example, if you want to participate in the instrumental music program you can join the band, the marching band, the orchestra, the jazz band, the pit orchestra (music played at a theatre production) or even a pep band which plays at sporting events. In art, you may want a drawing class, a painting class or maybe a pottery class. See what I'm talking about? Your options are limitless and you are sure to find something you like that is not offered at your home school. Theatre was my favorite and I not only joined our after-school drama club, but I auditioned and was picked to be in the chorus of an American musical production. If you are not gifted in the fine arts, don't worry because everybody is welcome. It is possible you will discover that you have talent that you just don't know about yet.

FACTS...

- America has many excellent summer fine arts camps for very talented kids of all ages and nationalities.
- Some fines arts classes (such as marching band or dance) can substitute for a physical education requirement.

STATE of the UNION

Utah State Capital - Salt Lake City

HOST PARENT

70 - i CRAZY

The Apple Company has taken America (and the world) by storm. First, let me explain that computers are used throughout the United States. Almost all schools and students utilize Apple computers, while almost all businesses and professionals use PCs. Second, it seems like every MP3 player is some sort of Apple iPod. Runners use an iPod Shuffle, novices utilize an iPod Nano and serious users own an iPod Touch. The top of the line product is the Apple iPhone, which is similar to a iTouch with a built in phone. These MP3 players and phones may not be anything new to you or much different than electronic items offered in your country, but in America these are the biggest sellers. Apple offers their exclusive MP3 store called itunes and provides these songs in a format typically not transferable to other formats. Don't let this stop you from bringing your MP3 player and besides, who can go without one these days? Wait, I didn't mention the iPad...I guess iCrazy.

DID YOU KNOW?

By April 9, 2007, 100 million iPods had been sold (in just 5 years). It is estimated that by the same date in 2009 over 150 million units had been sold. (38)

AMERICAN SLANG

I love my iPod but it cost me an "arm and a leg". (This is a typical way of saying something is expensive.)

EXCHANGE STUDENT

70 - i CRAZY

You might be wondering why this is even a topic in this book and I agree that when my host dad suggested it, I was a bit confused myself. Having spent almost a year in America I now completely understand. Almost everybody seems to have an MP3 player and many people have Apple iPods, but in America everybody seems to have an Apple iPod—kids, adults, students, teachers, parents and yes, even some grandparents. At school, computers are all Apple Mac's and believe it or not, they are actually more fun to use with their cool applications. When you come to America be ready to enter the world of Apple because you really don't have a choice. Here is a cool secret. If you want to spot an American in your country without hearing them talk, just look for the classic white ear buds connected to their Apple iPod; you can't miss it once you know what you are looking for.

FACTS...

- Most iPods are sold in various colors to match your personality.
- Various iPod types are available depending on your use or activity.
- Most iPods have various storage capacities and are large enough to hold even the largest of music libraries.
- Every year, more American schools are providing students with laptop computer and most school computers are made by Apple.

STATE of the UNION

Wisconsin Nickname - America's Dairyland

HOST PARENT

71 - RELATIONSHIPS

Oh no, do we have to talk about this subject? Here is the question of the year. Do you want to establish a romantic relationship with somebody while you are so far away from home when you will eventually be leaving? Your parents and your host parents will most likely hope that you do not, mostly because they both want you to enjoy everything else associated with your exchange year and not get too distracted from all there is to do at your new home and your new school. As we say in America, this may be easier said than done. You will be going to many parties, dances and team/club meetings where you will have plenty of opportunities to begin a romance. It certainly is possible to have a relationship and still not let it affect your school or your experience, but be warned about one important item. You will find that it is very hard to leave your new family when your year is over, so you can only imagine how difficult it will be to leave your boyfriend or girlfriend for what will most likely be forever.

DID YOU KNOW?

Did you know 47.8% of American students claim to have had sexual intercourse? This is extremely high and you don't want to become another statistic in America. (39)

AMERICAN SLANG

The teacher was not happy when she caught them "canoodling" in the hallway. (This describes physical affection such as kissing and hugging.)

STATE of the UNION

Louisiana State Capital - Baton Rouge

EXCHANGE STUDENT

71 - RELATIONSHIPS

My best friend from Norway had a relationship with another exchange student from Turkey, while a German exchange friend of mine had a pretty serious relationship with one of my American friends. Some of my friends from home in Germany had to leave their relationships behind while they did an exchange somewhere else in the world. Sounds pretty crazy I know, but actually everybody seemed fine with their own situation. I think that if both people know that their relationships may never be truly serious then go ahead and give it a try, but if you think it is something that may last forever then you may need to consider having fun other ways during your exchange year. I chose to not have a serious relationship during my year away, but that did not mean I did not go on a date or accept an invitation to homecoming or prom. You also need to consider your host family situation and what a relationship may mean to your siblings or parents. It could require more driving and will definitely take away some important family time. It is your decision, but make sure you think about all of the consequences.

TIPS...

- Remember your exchange year will come to an end. Keep that in mind when you leave a relationship behind or you are establishing one in America.
- Be polite to your host family when having a boyfriend or girlfriend over at your house. Consider their values and rules.
- When going on a date, make sure you are home when you are told or it may be your last date.
- Most American dates include a dinner and a movie.
- "Dating" is fine, but a serious "relationship" may have a bad effect on your social life during your time in America.

HOST PARENT

72 - YEARBOOK

Every middle school and high school in America publishes a yearbook at the end of the school year. This yearbook is a "professionally" bound and published book which is really nothing more than a very nice scrapbook. The book contains photographs of each sports team, club, group and organization and individual photographs of every student. Candid photographs taken at school and school events are often used in special sections that show both serious and fun things that occurred during the school year. You will also find a section with teacher and staff photos with a really nice color area of the yearbook devoted especially to the senior class. You can even join the "yearbook" club at the beginning of the year and work all year on its creation. The yearbook will be a great way for you to remember your time at your American high school and you will look back at it for the rest of your life.

DID YOU KNOW?

American schools take school pictures every year and sell them in different size packages to the students for giving to family and friends. Your photo will be included in the yearbook whether you want it or not, although you will not be required to purchase any of the photos.

AMERICAN SLANG

I'll always remember the fun times in high school by reading the "cheesy" comments written by my friends in my year book. (This could mean that something is silly or dumb.)

EXCHANGE STUDENT

72 - YEARBOOK

You are going to do so many things at your American school and you are going to meet so many people that it would be great if there was some way to remember it all. Well, there just happens to be a way and it's called a yearbook. At the beginning of the school year you will have your photo taken and you will pay about $50.00 U.S. dollars for the yearbook that you will receive at the end of the school year. This may seem expensive, but they are very large and they document just about every event that takes place during the school year. When the yearbooks arrive you are going to have great fun trying to find photos of yourself throughout the book and even more fun having your friends sign the yearbook. It is tradition to have your friends write a few nice or funny words so you can look back at them many years down the road.

FACTS...

- "Yearbook" is an elective class that students can take. Students are involved in many activities such as writing, photography, editing and organization.
- Working on the yearbook is like working for a magazine or a newspaper. Students are assigned activities or events and are then responsible for a story with words and pictures.

STATE of the UNION

Alaska Nickname - Last Frontier

HOST PARENT

73 - ALL NIGHT PARTY

I guess it is possible that some American high schools do not have such a party, but if there is one I have not found it (it is very possible that this is a regional activity). This is just one part of senior week that you are going to love. Every kid loves to stay up all night hanging out with their best friends. How about taking that to the next level? Why not have a party in your high school that lasts all night long and includes ALL of your senior friends? Furthermore, you can eat pizza, drink soda, play games and participate in all types of fun activities until you can hardly stand up anymore. At my all night party we even had side trips on the school bus to the roller skating rink and the bowling alley throughout the night and I still remember it like it was yesterday. You are not required to attend this party, but unless you are allergic to having fun, then you would be crazy to miss one of the highlights of the school year.

DID YOU KNOW?

Approximately 60% of children between the ages of 4-17 years old complained of being tired during the day. A survey conducted by the NSF determined that the average adult sleeps 6 hours and 58 minutes during the work week and that experts recommend 8 hours of sleep per night. (40)

AMERICAN SLANG

By 6:00 a.m. we were all acting "slap-happy"! (You must be acting crazy or strange because you have had little sleep.)

STATE of the UNION

New Hampshire State Capital - Concord

EXCHANGE STUDENT

73 - ALL NIGHT PARTY

The senior all night party was the coolest thing we did the week before graduation. Can you imagine spending all night with your friends at your school without classes and without teachers? It really is as fun as it sounds. You will most likely have to pay a little to attend the party, but most of the costs are covered by money earned at fund raisers and by local businesses who donate items for the party. The party will begin around 10:00 or 11:00 p.m. and end around 5:00 or 6:00 a.m. at which time you will be ready to come home and get some sleep. Parents usually run the event and they will have all kinds of fun activities planned. At our party there were all kinds of games set up in the gymnasium, including, basketball and volleyball. Our lunch room was set up like a casino and we were able to play games and win tickets that could be traded in for small prizes. The highlight of our night was a show put on by a hired hypnotist who was able to make students do crazy things that they would not normally do in front others. Do yourself a favor and go to this party.

TIPS...

- Go to bed early the night before the party so you will be well rested to stay up all night.
- It is not required and you might want to make sure all your friends are planning on attending.
- Don't play too many athletic games or you may get tired too quickly.
- Soda with caffeine may just be the trick to help stay awake all night.

HOST PARENT

74 - SENIOR WEEK

I think we got a little creative with the title of this topic since most schools may not officially have something called a "senior week". It does seem like an appropriate title for the week(s) following your last day of school when seniors have all kinds of cool things scheduled. Every school is different but you will most likely participate in an All Night Party, graduation rehearsal, senior breakfast and finish with a fantastic graduation ceremony. This is the week, or rather the time of year, that almost all high school kids have been working towards. It is the culmination of 13 years in school (including Kindergarten) and it is the beginning of the rest of your life. Having been through it myself I can say that it is the last weeks that you will see many of your classmates since everybody will be moving on to other things. This is even true for exchange students, so make sure you attend every event and get the most out of the last part of your senior year at your American high school.

DID YOU KNOW?

Did you know that seniors are usually done with school one or two weeks earlier than everybody else? This is so they can get started on summer work and/or prepare for college (university).

AMERICAN SLANG

I'm told that your senior year is a complete "blow-off" (It must be very easy.)

STATE of the UNION

South Carolina Nickname - Palmetto State

EXCHANGE STUDENT

74 - SENIOR WEEK

Being a senior in an American high school is something really special. At first I was curious why all exchange students were classified as "Seniors" even though most of us should be juniors based on our age and education level (usually 11th year). After being in the United States for a year, I now know why; because being a senior in an American high school is even more fun than just being in an American high school. Apparently Americans want us to have the full experience! Even many adults I met in America still reminisce about their senior year in high school and talk about it like it was yesterday. My senior week was as my American friends like to say—icing on the cake. In other words, it was the best experience of an already fantastic time. Now imagine that you will also be heading home soon, so this week may also include other fun stuff like exchange student parties and get-togethers with your best friends. Unfortunately, it is also a time of mixed emotions. You will be celebrating and having fun, you will be tired and stressed and will possibility be upset about your coming departure for home. It will be crazy, so hold on and enjoy the ride.

TIPS...

- Some of these activities may cost a little bit.
- Your host parents may be working during senior week so make plans for rides to and from events.
- Take your yearbook to these events because it is a great time to have them signed by your friends.
- This is a great time to buy a new outfit for graduation.
- Still get plenty of rest; you don't want to be sick during the last few weeks/days of your stay in America.

HOST PARENT

75 - GRADUATION

This is the last topic in this chapter as well as the last chapter of your stay in America. For Americans, it honors the achievement of 13 long years in school. For you, it honors your achievement of a successful year as an exchange student in your American high school. Both are reasons to celebrate for you, your exchange student friends and your American senior classmates. As an American parent, I can say that it is a time of recognition and a time of change. It is the time when your child finishes mandatory school and moves on to college, which usually coincides with leaving the house and making their own way in life. As the host parent of an exchange student, I must admit I felt the same way. I was extremely proud of what she had accomplished in school, especially her unbelievable command of the English language. My exchange daughter arrived a shy teenage girl and she left a confident young woman. She truly graduated and is ready to take on the world.

DID YOU KNOW?

Did you know "*Pomp and Circumstance*" is a march (song) played for the procession at every American graduation (high school and college)? Everybody in America knows the music, but it is not even American. It was written in 1905 by Sir Edward Elgar of England for the coronation of King Edward the VII.

AMERICAN SLANG

It's a "bummer" that I may never see some of my classmates ever again. (This is another way of say that you are sad.)

STATE of the UNION

Michigan State Capital - Lansing

EXCHANGE STUDENT

75 - GRADUATION

This will be the last official American school event you will attend. It will be happy, sad, exciting and fun all at the same time. This is the goal of every American high school student and it will be the highlight of your exchange year. You may celebrate the completion of school in your country, but you probably will not take it to the extreme that they do in America. Let me explain. First, you will receive what is called a "cap and gown" which is the attire that you will wear on graduation day (a robe in school colors and a square hat with a tassel, just as you've seen in the movies). Next, you will have to go to graduation rehearsal so nobody messes up during the big event that will be attended by parents, relatives and close friends. The graduation ceremony will be held at a huge auditorium, gymnasium or even at the football field. Finally, each and every graduating senior will get their turn in the spotlight. You will walk across the stage when your name is called and you will receive your high school degree (or certificate of achievement for us exchange students). The day will be finished with either a party or a nice dinner out with your family and relatives. This is a day you will not soon forget.

TIPS...

- There will be a small cost for your cap and gown.
- Charge your camera battery and make sure your memory card has room for all the graduation photos.
- Your graduation may be webcast, make sure you tell your parents about it back home.
- Decorate the top of your cap so family and friends can find you in the huge crowd of graduates.

Dominique's school in America

Marching band

Ready for Homecoming Dance

CHAPTER 4

HOLIDAYS AND FREE TIME

HOST PARENT

76 - LABOR DAY

This will be the first American holiday that you will experience, because it is always the first Monday in September and will most likely be soon after your arrival in the United States. Labor Day is a holiday *"—dedicated to the social and economic achievement of American workers."* as defined by the U.S. Department of Labor. The American school year generally begins near Labor Day and it typically marks the end of summer vacation for American students. Summer vacation is generally defined as the time between Memorial Day (end of May) and Labor Day (beginning of September). Labor Day is usually celebrated outdoors with activities such as camping, boating, picnicking or just getting together with friends and family. This will be your first chance to meet friends of your host family and no matter what activity you find yourself doing, I am sure you are going to have a great time at the beginning of a great school year.

DID YOU KNOW?

Schools across America will start anywhere from the second week of August to the week after Labor Day. They will end anywhere from Memorial Day weekend to the end of June. Check the calendar of your new American high school to find out when you will begin and end.

AMERICAN SLANG

Labor Day will be your last chance to "chill" before the school year begins. (This is to relax and do nothing or just hanging out is another term used by Americans.)

STATE of the UNION

Arkansas Nickname - Natural State

EXCHANGE STUDENT

76 - LABOR DAY

My very first weekend in the United States was a holiday. Labor Day marks the beginning of the American school year and this will probably be your first holiday here, too. No matter where you are in America, it will probably still be very warm outside and most Americans use this holiday as their last get-away of the summer. My host family took me to Lake Michigan where we spent the day swimming and sunbathing. After spending an entire beautiful day on the beach we visited family nearby and barbequed, played games and went boating and swimming in the lake. It was a great way to kick off the year and an even better way to meet family and begin practicing my English conversation skills.

FACTS...

This is an official list of U.S. Holidays and many of them will get you some time off of school:

- January 1, New Years Day
- January 19, Martin Luther King's Birthday
- February (3rd Monday), President's Day
- May (Last Monday), Memorial Day
- July 4, Independence Day
- September (1st Monday), Labor Day
- October (2nd Monday), Columbus Day
- November (4th Thursday), Thanksgiving
- December 25, Christmas Day

HOST PARENT

77 - PARKS and RECREATION

The first place we visited with our exchange student was a park. We got to know each other while riding bikes and enjoying the sun and the water. America is a land of parks, both big and small. My favorite places to visit are those established by the National Park System and include wonderful places like Yellowstone National Park in Wyoming, Rocky Mountain National Park in Colorado, and Everglades National Park in Florida. These are places of incredible beauty and natural wonders that are found in many areas across the United States. Each of America's 50 States has their own State Park System where you can do everything from fishing and hiking to swimming, biking and camping. Most likely you will find yourself living not too far from a State Park or a National Park and that is just the beginning. This land of parks also includes wonderful places operated by counties, cities and villages. You may even think that many of our schools can be considered parks because of all the ball fields and activities available at these locations.

DID YOU KNOW?

Parks can be defined as something of natural geographic beauty or as simple as a place for recreation such as camping, hiking or swimming. The United States has 9,161,966 square kilometers of land and 664,709 square kilometers of water which means there is a lot of room for parks and recreation. (41)

AMERICAN SLANG

I missed the day at the park because I was feeling "under the weather." (This means that you don't feel very good.)

EXCHANGE STUDENT

77 - PARKS and RECREATION

Parks, parks, parks and more parks. In Europe we think of a park as a grassy area with benches and a water fountain. These are beautiful and relaxing, but in America they not only have those parks, but parks of all kinds. They have parks of natural wonder and beauty like the Mammoth Caves (underground caves) or Sequoia (largest trees in the world), and parks for exercise where you can run, bike, roller blade or play outdoor sports. Many other parks have outdoor recreational activities like hiking, backpacking, mountain climbing, fishing, hunting and much more. During my year in America, I spent time in many such parks. We hiked into the Grand Canyon, we swam in one of the largest freshwater lakes in the world (Lake Michigan), we rode bikes on trails near our home and we even had my farewell party at a beautiful county park in my host city. You are never far from a park of some sort. Make sure you go at every opportunity.

FACTS...

Facts about the American National Park Service: (42)

- The NPS administers 394 areas (including parks, monuments, seashores, etc.)
- The NPS has over 84 million acres of land in every state except Delaware.
- Yellowstone was the first National Park established in 1872 by President Ulysses S. Grant and the Park Service was established in 1916 by President Woodrow Wilson.
- In 2009, the NPS had 285,579,941 visitors with only 20,500 employees.

STATE of the UNION

Colorado State Capital - Denver

HOST PARENT

78 - BEACH

The first time we left town with our exchange daughter it was off to the beach for the whole family. Throughout the year we made several other trips to the beach. You might be lucky enough to find a home near a beautiful ocean beach, but if you don't, there is no need to fret. Beaches are everywhere throughout America, because there are rivers, lakes and oceans all around you. Yes, you heard me right—I said oceans (plural): The Atlantic Ocean, Pacific Ocean, Gulf of Mexico and the beautiful Caribbean Sea. Because you will be arriving in August and you will not be leaving until sometime in June, you will have plenty of beach weather everywhere in America. Just because you might live in the middle of America does not mean that you won't get to enjoy a beach. Inland lakes are everywhere and public beaches can be found at many State and local parks. So put on your bathing suit, lather up with plenty of sunscreen, grab your sunglasses, slide into your flip-flops and head for the beach.

DID YOU KNOW?

- Michigan has more shoreline than any other State except Alaska (check it out).
- You can find beautiful black sand beaches in Hawaii (formed from lava rock).
- Minnesota has 11,842 lakes, but still cannot compare to Alaska's 3 million lakes.
- Wherever you go in Florida you are never more than 60 miles from a beach.

STATE of the UNION

Virginia Nickname - Old Dominion

EXCHANGE STUDNET

78 - BEACH

I love the beach and, fortunately, so did my host family. Two days after I arrived in America we spent the day at Lake Michigan, but that was just the beginning. On my first day of school there was a beach party for the new exchange students and it took place at one of the thousands of small lakes found throughout Michigan. Many people in America live at a lake, own a boat and spend plenty of time in and on the water. Even if you don't get the chance to water ski or go tubing, you will get plenty of opportunities to sun bathe and build sand castles. Don't worry if there's no beach close to your exchange home, I have never seen so many private pools and hot tubs as I did during my exchange year (even in a cold state like Michigan). My biggest beach adventure was a trip to Daytona Beach, Florida. It was a bit cold in November, but I went into the water anyway just so I could say that I swam in the Atlantic Ocean.

TIPS...

- Don't forget your bathing suit. Modesty is recommended in America.
- Your host family will have plenty of beach towels.
- Your host family will have sunscreen, but if you have special SPF (sun protection factor) needs, then bring yours.
- Sunglasses and flip-flops are a must!

AMERICAN SLANG

The sunset over the ocean will "knock your socks off".
(This means that something was absolutely fantastic.)

HOST PARENT

79 - AMUSEMENT PARKS

Everybody loves amusement parks and almost everybody has visited amusement parks in their own country. Americans are no different, but just like everything else in America—amusement parks are big and rides are often even bigger. Take for example Walt Disney World (Florida), it has four huge theme parks and two water parks. These parks are a very popular vacation destination and you may get the opportunity to visit with your host family. If you aren't as lucky as our host daughter, don't worry, you can always find an amusement park somewhat close to your host house. Six Flags has amusement parks all over the country or you can find specialty parks like Sea World or smaller (but just as fun) independent parks. Finally, during the summer and autumn months don't forget to attend a "county fair" (or carnival) that often has traveling shows, games and amusement rides. You will find plenty of times and locations to get dizzy, go fast and hang upside down.

DID YOU KNOW?

According to ultimaterollercoaster.com, Russians began the craze with Ice Slides which were huge wooden structures for sleds that eventually evolved into carts with wheels.

AMERICAN SLANG

I was feeling "iffy" about riding the new huge rollercoaster. (Iffy mean that you are not sure or you have mixed feelings about doing something.)

EXCHANGE STUDENT

79 - AMUSEMENT PARKS

After standing in line for one and a half hours watching people take a rollercoaster ride straight up into the sky then come straight back towards the ground, it was finally our turn to experience this thrill. That's right, after waiting 5,400 seconds it was our opportunity to take a 17 second ride directly up 420 feet (130 meters) and straight back down at 120 miles per hour (193 kilometers per hour). Was I scared? You bet, and so will you if you have the nerve to strap yourself into this rocket. This thrill was experienced at Cedar Point Amusement Park located in Sandusky, Ohio, on a peninsula in Lake Erie. Cedar Point is known as the "Rollercoaster Capital of the World" and it lives up to its name with 17 of them. Because of my host dad and brother, I am now addicted to thrill rides. If you find yourself weak in the stomach don't worry, these parks have plenty of easier rides, games and shows. It is impossible to have a bad time at any amusement park.

FACTS...

- There are 21 "Six Flags" amusement parks throughout North America.
- Cedar Point, in Ohio, has more roller coasters than any other single amusement park.
- According to Disney, they employ over 50,000 people in Walt Disney World, Orlando, Florida

STATE of the UNION

South Dakota State Capital - Pierre

HOST PARENT

80 - FRIENDS

You will learn and see numerous things during your stay in America, many of which we have tried to share with you in this book. The greatest thing you are going to take home from this trip cannot be purchased and it cannot be learned. It will be the most valuable possession you take home—friendship. A good friend is a friend forever and memories you create with them are yours to cherish as the highlight of your exchange trip. Ludwig van Beethoven summed it up best when he said *"Never shall I forget the days I spent with you. Continue to be my friend, and I shall always be yours."* Our exchange student arrived in America with two suitcases and memories of her friends at home. She went back home with two suitcases and memories of new friends from America and all over the world. You can never pack too many friends in your life, so get ready to meet many new people...they may be your friends for a long, long time.

DID YOU KNOW?

Facebook is America's fastest growing computer social networking site. According to Facebook there are currently (2011) over 500 million users and the average user has 130 friends. (43)

AMERICAN SLANG

I'm hanging out with my "posse" at the mall today. (Kids use this term to refer to a group of their friends.)

STATE of the UNION

North Carolina Nickname - First in Flight

EXCHANGE STUDENT

80 - FRIENDS

Leaving my friends for ten months was difficult, but traveling to a different country and making new friends seemed like an even bigger challenge. It was much easier than I thought, because my host siblings and family introduced me to many people. Student government had a welcome party for exchange students and the American kids are overall very friendly and welcoming. You will quickly become friends with other exchange students who are also new to your school and you may find they become some of your best friends. I met most of my friends by participating in sports and clubs where you become "team" members all having the same goal, regardless of what country you are from—at my school we were ALL pirates and at yours you may be tigers or dragons or who knows what. Finally, and I must admit, the most fun...you will be treated like a movie star. The American students love meeting and talking to the foreign exchange students and it quickly adds friends to your Facebook page. Don't be shy and you will fit in perfectly with the typical friendly and outgoing American.

TIPS...

- Be like the Americans—don't be shy and introduce yourself to many people.
- Be proud of being an exchange student and use this as your topic of introduction.
- Make friends with other exchange students.
- Use every opportunity to hang out with your friends because your time will go by fast.

HOST PARENT

81 - HALLOWEEN

This is a European tradition that has, in many ways, taken its own form in the United States. Traditionally, Halloween represents "All Hallows Eve", or the eve of All Saints Day. Many years ago this was a day of mischief caused mostly by young kids looking for trouble and finding Halloween an excuse to make "tricks". Near the middle of the 19th century communities began giving "treats" to youngsters and through the years this evolved into a custom we call "trick or treating". Children of all ages dress up in fun and scary costumes and walk door-to-door calling out "trick or treat", while adults enjoy looking at all the costumes and rewarding the kids with a treat—usually a sweet of some kind. This is not a formal holiday and kids still go to school on this day, but be prepared to see vampires, princesses and werewolves in each classroom.

DID YOU KNOW?

It is said that Ancient Celtic people wore costumes to confuse the spirits who were thought to roam the earth as they traveled to the afterlife the night before Samham (now called All Saints Day or All Hallows Day). (44)

AMERICAN SLANG

I have never seen so many "corny" costumes in one place before. (Corny is used often and it means something that is funny or goofy looking.)

EXCHANGE STUDENT

81 - HALLOWEEN

Dia de los muertos. That is Spanish for Halloween and I learned it in school on October 31. Halloween has a long tradition in the United States (and North America) and everything that day is about Halloween. It starts at school, where lots of students and staff dress up as scary, weird or just funny characters. In most classes, you do get a break from the usual work and do something fun that has to do with Halloween. We watched a movie about the history of Halloween in U.S. History class. We played Halloween games in math class and we celebrated "el dia de los muertos" in Spanish class where we made sugar skulls. At dusk, we went trick or treating with a huge group of students, while adults passed out candy to all who participated. It is a really large party for all ages and everybody has a whole bunch of fun and you will most certainly end up with a whole bunch of great American candy (and possibly a new cavity in a tooth).

TIPS...

- The average American will spend approximately $66.00 on costumes, candy, decorations and greeting cards. (45)
- Every year the most popular costumes include: witch, pirate, vampire and princess.
- In 2007, the average American consumed 24.5 pounds of candy, mostly at Halloween. The estimated number of trick-or-treaters in the same year was 36.1 million (kids age 5-13). (46)

STATE of the UNION

Maryland State Capital - Annapolis

HOST PARENT

82 - HAUNTED HOUSES/CIDER MILLS

My favorite season is autumn (more commonly called "fall" in America), not just because of the beautiful color changes in our part of the country, but also because of the many activities that take place this time of year. Cider mills may be in your country too, but in America going to a cider mill is a tradition that nobody misses. Although the cider mills are packed with people, there are many things you can do. With our exchange daughter, we took a hay ride, picked our own apples and had a great picnic eating warm cinnamon doughnuts and fresh apple cider. Many cider mills have farm animals for the little kids and corn mazes for people of all ages to enjoy. You don't know what a corn maze is? See the "Did you know?" section for more information. Finally, your trip to the cider mill will not be complete without walking through the pumpkin patch and choosing your pumpkins to be carved into jack-o-lanterns. Halloween is almost here and your cider mill visit will kick-off the season. Autumn is also great for other activities like football, trick-or-treating (see Halloween) and everybody's favorite pastime...haunted houses. Get ready to scream because everybody does!

DID YOU KNOW?

Originally maize (corn) was a grass the Aztecs (native people) domesticated into what we know as corn. Mazes made in corn fields have become extremely popular in North America and you will find them wherever corn in grown. Did you know another English word for corn is maize and so you could actually call these a Maize Maze (pronounced the same)?

STATE of the UNION

Indiana Nickname - Hoosier State

EXCHANGE STUDENT

82 - HAUNTED HOUSES/CIDER MILLS

When Halloween gets close, many people will decorate their homes just like it was Christmas, except they use orange lights and they will hang up ghosts, goblins and scary creatures around their yard. For several weeks before October 31st, you can find "haunted houses" in just about every city. This is an extremely popular thing for kids of all ages to do, but mostly you will find that high school students are the ones crazy enough to do this activity. Imagine a very large house or an old abandoned warehouse or even some very dark woods. If you have that picture in your head, now think about going in at night with your friends and finding the zombies, monsters, and bloody scenes that you usually see in horror movies. Here's the best (or scariest) thing—almost all the creatures and bodies in the haunted house are real and their objective is to scare you to death...and they do a really good job of that. My town had a "Terrified Forest" and the last thing I remember was being chased down a trail by a bloody guy with a chain saw! Ahhhhhhhhh! Don't be afraid...just do it!

TIPS...

- Always go to a haunted house with a group of friends because you can go in together.
- Try not to be the first person in your group to go into the haunted house...you'll be the target.
- Make sure you have the hot cinnamon doughnuts at the cider mill, they're the best.
- Picking your own apples is much more fun, plus you have a snack while working.

AMERICAN SLANG

I'm not going with you because those places give me the "heebiegeebies". (They give you a creepy or scared feeling.)

HOST PARENT

83 - THANKSGIVING

There are only several other countries besides the United States to celebrate the harvest season with a holiday called Thanksgiving. In America, it is always celebrated on the last Thursday in November and typically consists of spending time with your family and enjoying a traditional Turkey dinner garnished with stuffing, mashed potatoes, pumpkin pie and many other delicious foods. School is always closed on Thursday and Friday of this week and it comes at a perfect time in the school year for a little break. Most people stay home or visit nearby relatives and take a short rest before winter moves in for a long stay. In recent years Thanksgiving has become better known as the "beginning" of the Christmas season. Thousands of Americans head for the shopping malls on Friday morning (commonly called "black Friday") after Thanksgiving since every store opens early (approximately 5:00 a.m.) and offers discounts so low that you can only find them on this one day of the year.

DID YOU KNOW?

It is estimated that 242 million turkeys were raised in the United States in 2010. That is approximately 7.1 billion pounds with an estimated value of 3.6 billion U.S. dollars. (47) Chances are you will soon be eating turkey.

AMERICAN SLANG

Every American "pigs out" on Thanksgiving. (To pig out means to eat way too much food.)

EXCHANGE STUDENT

83 - THANKSGIVING

Most American kids learn about the history of Thanksgiving when they are very young so I did my own investigation. According to my American classmates, it appears that the very first Thanksgiving took place between Native Americans and the early European settlers in an area of the United States called New England (NE America). It is also widely believed that various groups of Native Americans have always been celebrating and worshiping during the autumn harvest season. You will observe young students bringing home Pilgrim and turkey art projects to hang on the refrigerator and a lot of happy school kids getting a long weekend away from the classroom. This may be your first opportunity to meet cousins, uncles, aunts and grandparents of your host family during your stay. Enjoy, have fun and save room for the pumpkin pie...if you have not yet enjoyed this desert—you will!

TIPS...

- A male turkey is called a Tom and a female turkey is called a hen.
- Turkey is low in fat and high in protein.
- Cranberries are traditionally served at Thanksgiving dinner and are said to have been served at the first Pilgrim feast.

AMERICAN SLANG

Nebraska State Capital - Lincoln

HOST PARENT

84 - CHRISTMAS and NEW YEAR

This was probably the most exciting time for me as a host parent. Christmas, more than any other time of the year, is when families can spend quality time together. Having another child to share Christmas with was special and something that our family will not forget. It is difficult to explain what you may experience since America is so large and so culturally diverse, but there is a good chance it will be just like ours. Visiting family, eating good food (usually turkey, ham or maybe like us—a Christmas goose) attending midnight service at church and exchanging gifts are just part of the festivities. Like in our country, New Years Eve and New Years Day are celebrated to escort out the old and celebrate the new. Most people will be found watching the "ball drop" in NYC's Time Square and toasting the New Year with Champagne and good luck kisses all around.

DID YOU KNOW?

It is estimated that over one million people attend the "ball dropping" in New York City's Time Square. At 11:59 p.m. on December 31 of each year a 12 foot crystal ball makes a "drop" to signify the New Year and if you are not there you are most likely watching it on television.

AMERICAN SLANG

Christmas in America is "over the top"! (This means that something is exaggerated and crazy.)

EXCHANGE STUDENT

84 - CHRISTMAS and NEW YEAR

Let me be clear, if you are away from home during your birthday (which is possible) and Christmas (which is probable) then you will no doubt come down with a quick case of home sickness. These are times that are important to you and your family, but that doesn't mean that you can't have fun and enjoy a new experience. For me, Christmas was only slightly different, while for some exchange students, it may be significantly different and for others it may be a completely new experience depending on their religion. Christmas Eve is mostly reserved for church and big family gatherings while your host family will likely do their gift exchange on Christmas morning. ... and if you have younger exchange siblings then plan on getting up early (real early). Also plan on a several week break from school while your first semester comes to an end and you prepare for the second half of your exchange school year.

FACTS...

- At midnight on the morning on New Year's Day, American's "toast" with Champagne.
- Following the "toast" it is good luck to kiss people near you, blow party horns and watch fireworks.
- Most Americans watch the "glass ball" drop in NYC Times Square at 12:00 a.m. on New Year's Day.

STATE of the UNION

California Nickname - Golden State

HOST PARENT

85 - SHOPPING MALLS

When writing this book, we tried not to read each other's pages before we completed our own, but that didn't always happen (as in the case of this shopping mall section). My exchange student is correct; you need to be a female to truly enjoy a shopping mall. I dislike malls with a passion, but that should not come as a surprise to you, as most men do not like shopping and malls are nothing more than a shopping nightmare. Can you imagine shopping in one store and when you leave the store you are literally 25 to 50 feet from the entrance to another store? If you have not visited the United States, it is quite possible that you have not had this experience and I do recommend it to everybody. Why, you ask? So you can say you did it and so you can quickly decide to never do it again! For those of you brave enough to give it a try, but quickly find it unappealing, it is good to know there are also restaurants in which to eat, or even seats where you can sit and watch some television while the girls in your party are off in shopping heaven.

DID YOU KNOW?

The Mall of America (Bloomington, Minnesota) is 4.2 million square feet, has 520 stores, employs 11,000 people and if a shopper spent 10 minutes browsing in every store it would take them more than 86 hours to complete their visit. (48)

AMERICAN SLANG

I found this "bling" at my favorite store in the mall. (Bling is usually a flashy, expensive clothing accessory.)

EXCHANGE STUDENT

85 - SHOPPING MALLS

Before my trip to America I was not really interested in shopping and I had only been to a few malls. Now that I have experienced the huge malls in America, I sure am going to miss them. Of course, since I am a girl, it would not be fair to say that all readers of this book are going to enjoy them as much as I did, but if you like shopping, you will most definitely love the mall. They will overload your senses with sights, smells and plenty of fine textures to add to your collection. It is a great activity to do with your friends and I often spent an entire day shopping, eating and gossiping with my friends (you can do it all without leaving the mall). In American malls you can find hundreds of stores in one huge building. Malls are beautiful at Christmas time with bright lights, wonderful decorations and even visits from Santa Claus, but beware of the crowds and lines during this time of year which can also be very frustrating. I heard rumors that a mall is being built near my home in Germany. That is just what I need for my new shopping addiction.

TIPS...

- You never have to leave a mall. Food, beverages and even entertainment can be found inside most malls. You could plan on an entire day.
- Go early. Before Christmas, malls can be so crowded it can be hard to find a parking spot.
- Many young adults spend an entire day at the mall to meet and hang out with friends.

STATE of the UNION

Iowa State Capital - Des Moines

HOST PARENT

86 - VACATIONS

This is a tough subject since everybody is completely different in regards to how they use their vacation time. Many Americans travel, while just as many or more do not. Some people use this time to catch up on chores around the house or others may use the time to do nothing except rest. It is not unusual, because families live in different areas of the country (since America is so huge) and it often requires that families use vacation time to visit their relatives. Whether you are visiting relatives of your host family or just lounging around the house, you will not be in school and all students find ways to fill their vacation with fun. Besides the ever popular three or four-day weekend, you will also experience several weeks of vacation during Christmas and New Year and another week of vacation during Easter. Take advantage of this time. If trips become available to you then you should take advantage of the opportunity to see as much of America as possible.

DID YOU KNOW?

Most Americans vacation during the summer months (June to August), while some take time off between Christmas and New Years or over Spring Break/Easter.

AMERICAN SLANG

We are going to vacation at the beach so we can "catch some rays".
(This is sun bathing, which is lying out in the sun.)

STATE of the UNION

Washington Nickname - Evergreen State

EXCHANGE STUDENT

86 - VACATIONS

If you like to travel, make sure that you write that in your student profile. My host family loves to travel and I was told that it made a difference in their selection. It can't hurt, but keep in mind that providing this information is no guarantee that you will go on a long distance trip. I have met many students from America who have never traveled outside of their own state, but there are just as many who have. I was lucky since during my ten months in America I was able to travel to eleven states from Michigan to Florida and from Virginia to California and visit such cool places as Disney World, Washington, D.C. and the Grand Canyon. But don't worry, even if you don't get to travel that much you will surely be vacationing somewhere in your own State and visiting places you've never seen before.

FACTS...

The top 10 most visited U.S. tourist sites are (2010): (49)

1. Times Square - New York, New York
2. Las Vegas - Nevada
3. National Mall & Memorial Parks - Washington D.C.
4. Faneuil Hall Marketplace - Boston, Massachusetts
5. Disney World - Orlando, Florida
6. Golden Gate Park - San Francisco, California
7. Disneyland - Anaheim, California
8. Fisherman's Warf - San Francisco, California
9. Hollywood Walk of Fame - Los Angeles, California
10. Great Smokey Mountains - Tennessee

HOST PARENT

87 - TELEVISION

Of course you can watch television (TV), doesn't everybody? The whole world is hooked on television these days, although I've always figured America was the most addicted, but I'll let you decide that by yourself. Whenever I take a walk at night through our neighborhood, I can always count on seeing the glowing lights of television sets as I walk by each home. Although I make TV sound like a bad thing, I think in the case of an American home with an exchange student that television can be a really good thing. The television provides great family time where you can watch the national and local news, check out the popular culture and get a continuous stream of that English language you came here to conquer. It will also help that you will be entertained at the same time. We even found that some of the shows are the same shows you watch at home, only they are with different hosts and speaking a different language. So get a blanket, find your favorite chair and settle in for a relaxing evening of American television.

DID YOU KNOW?

Americans are watching television more than ever. A May, 2009 survey showed that the average American watches 153 hours of TV at home each month. That is an average of just over 5 hours per day. Wow! (50)

AMERICAN SLANG

I like TV, but some people are just terrible "couch potatoes". (This is a person who never leaves the couch.)

STATE of the UNION

Idaho State Capital - Boise

EXCHANGE STUDENT

87 - TELEVISION

Americans do watch TV a lot, but I'm not sure they watch any more than you do. If they do watch more television it is probably because they have more TVs. I actually had my own television in my bedroom and so did my host sister, my host brother, my host parents and most of my exchange friends. If that is not enough, we had a huge 60 inch (152.4 centimeters) TV in our basement "movie" room. It was just like having your own personal movie theater. You will be surprised to see some of the same television shows that you watch at home that are either the same show (in English) or a show that has a very similar theme (like American Idol). Sitcoms (situation comedies) are very popular in America and most families have one or two they like to watch every week. Did you know that most schools (school districts) have their own television station (on cable TV) where you can watch your high school sports or special presentations? Of course, your local school TV station is best used for early mornings when they post whether or not school is closed due to weather or other reasons. But the best thing about TV in the U.S. is that it is a great way to spend quality time with your American host family.

TIPS...

- TV is fun and entertaining, but never let it interfere with your homework or take place of a better activity like a school club.
- Most of the popular TV shows come on at what Americans call "Prime Time" (8:00 p.m. till 11:00 p.m.)
- Do not snack too much while watching television. This may be one reason Americans are said to be fat!
- If you need extra help with your English skills, turn on the closed captioning while watching television.

HOST PARENT

88 - WINTER FUN

Who picked this topic? Is there any fun in winter? It is my theory that winter fun is relative to your age. In other words, the older you get the more you dislike winter, but that does not mean that I don't have many great memories of winter fun. Building snow forts, finding the best hidden sledding hills or best of all, staying home when school is closed because there is too much snow for the school busses to make it to your house! Yes, snow can be fun and if you have not experienced snow or if you live in a place that receives only a little bit...well, you just might end up in a place that will remind you of the North Pole. There are always two sides to every story and the ugly side includes things like slippery and dangerous driving conditions, grey skies and don't forget that snow down your pants is always an unpleasant experience. You may be lucky (in my opinion) and end up in a nice warm winter place or at the very least maybe you will take a mid-winter vacation to a warm part of the United States.

DID YOU KNOW?

December 22nd is the first day of winter for all locations in the northern hemisphere and it is the shortest day of the year for daylight. If you end up in some locations in Alaska you may only see the sun for three hours!

AMERICAN SLANG

My host dad gets so "ornery" in the cold winter weather. (He must be irritated, unhappy and upset!)

STATE of the UNION

Kentucky Nickname - Bluegrass State

EXCHANGE STUDENT

88 - WINTER FUN

Depending on what country you come from will most likely determine whether you feel lucky or unlucky if you get placed with a family from the northern parts of the United States. Winter in Michigan was a new experience for me with temperatures rarely above 32 degrees (0 degrees Celsius) and a whole lot of snow. Although my host family has seen enough snow over the years, I could not get enough of it and when we got the first snow of the year (early November), we all went directly outside and made a snowman. There are many fun winter activities such as snowball fights, tobogganing, sledding, ice skating, skiing and snowboarding. Don't let the cold temperatures scare you, once you're outside having fun you will forget all about the lack of feeling in your toes. If you find yourself in a warm climate I am sure you will enjoy decorating palm trees with Christmas lights and going to the beach in shorts in December...something I unfortunately missed.

TIPS...

GO OUT

- Ice Skating, sledding, tobogganing, skIIng, snowboarding, cross country skiing, hockey, building snowmen, building snow forts and having snowball fights

STAY IN

- Bowling, roller skating, movies/cinema, parties, sleepovers, gymnasium and indoor swimming pools and water parks.

HOST PARENT

89 - MOVIES

It does not matter where you live in the United States, most Americans love going to the movies. You can find a movie theatre in almost any size town...you can probably find a small screen theatre in a barn or the world's largest screens at IMAX theatres. Most larger cities or suburbs have large multiplexes or megaplexes which are locations that have multiple movie screens—in some cases up to 26 screens! If there is a movie you have wanted to see, then you're are going to have plenty of chances during your stay in America, wherever you may be. Movie theatres throughout America are gathering places for school-age kids and there are always new movies being released every weekend. It is also a great place to meet up with friends from your school or other area schools and catch up on things or even play a video game or two if you happen to live near a megaplex. Have fun and don't forget the popcorn and Milk Duds...oh you don't know about American snacks yet? You will soon.

DID YOU KNOW?

In 2009 there were approximately 1.4 billion theatre admissions in the U.S. and Canada. That is approximately 4 ticket sales per person in both countries. (51)

AMERICAN SLANG

That was a fantastic "flick". (A flick is a movie.)

EXCHANGE STUDENT

89 - MOVIES

Americans are CRAZY for movies. Most families live within several miles of a movie theatre and many of them have a big screen TV with a very impressive DVD collection. This included my host family and most of my American friends. My definition of an American party includes the usual hanging with friends, enjoying pizza and pop (soda). Typically the party will include a good (and sometimes bad) movie. Going to the movie theatre is a normal activity and it is not unusual to go once a week. During my ten months in the United States I have seen more movies than in the first 16 years of my life prior to my exchange. I was really not into movies before I arrived but now I am addicted and this is one addiction I plan on keeping. Hundreds of movies are made in America and you don't have to be in Hollywood to be in one. Check the Internet for casting calls and you may find yourself as an "extra" in a big movie as I did...I bet you can't spot the German girl in the new "High School" movie but if you do I would be happy to sign an autograph.

TIPS...

- There are approximately 39,000 movie screens throughout the U.S. (52)
- There are still approximately 600 drive-in theatres throughout America (movies to watch from your car). (52)
- Seating in American theaters is not assigned—it is open admission.

STATE of the UNIION

Delaware State Capital - Dover

HOST PARENT

90 - CONCERTS

Everybody loves concerts and you will have opportunities galore in the United States. You may not think that America is a very "cultural" place, but you are in for a big surprise. There are extremely talented people in America and many of them make a living in the arts and entertainment industry. I love the huge concerts by international stars that often take place in outdoor theatres during the summer time, but I also like the small local concerts performed by new or young artists. Because America is such a huge sports loving country, there are unlimited locations for concerts of all sizes. We have football and baseball stadiums for summer concerts and basketball and hockey arenas for winter concerts. Additionally, there are concert halls, outdoor amphitheatres and college facilities everywhere that provide locations for culture every single day of the year. And let's not forget about theatre and the ever popular American musical. We took our exchange daughter to a popular musical in Chicago and multiple concerts in local towns by our home. That is just the beginning, how about concerts at your American high school and your chance to participate.

DID YOU KNOW?

Eight of the top ten most attended concerts in history have taken place in America. The largest was the New York Philharmonic Orchestra in NYC's Central Park and the most famous happened in 1969 at Woodstock in Bethel, NY. (53)

STATE of the UNION

Georgia Nickname - Peach State

AMERICAN SLANG

By the time the concert was over, I was "running on empty" (This mean you are worn out and have no energy left.)

EXCHANGE STUDENT

90 - CONCERTS

There really is no way to avoid concerts or other performances during your stay in America and more than likely you may even be participating in one or more of these events. During my year I watched my host sister perform in concert band and my host brother perform in jazz band, while both of my siblings played in the marching band at every home football game. I also saw friends perform in choir concerts and my family and friends all came to see me perform in the class musical (every American high school does a musical and several plays throughout the year). These were just performances at my high school. My host family would also take me to see local musicians perform at small concert halls and I had opportunities to see international stars with friends when they came to the local arenas and stadiums. My favorite performance activity was during a trip to Chicago where we were able to see the touring Broadway musical "Wicked". Getting dressed up and spending this musical evening with my family and friends was truly a highlight of my exchange year.

TIPS...

- Big cities offer the most opportunities for international artists. These may set you back $50.00 to $100.00 each.
- Ask your host parents to assist in purchasing tickets for reduced rates such as AAA or other discounts.
- Local concerts are much more affordable and can range from $15.00 to $30.00.
- Find a group of friends that want to go and assist with transportation and split up gas/parking costs.

HOST PARENT

91 - BIRTHDAYS

Everybody celebrates their birthday and chances are that you will be celebrating one of your birthdays in America. It is also likely that you will be around for birthdays of your host family. If that is not enough to celebrate, we even celebrate the birthdays of famous historical people in America like Martin Luther King, Jr. Most schools are closed for several days in February to celebrate "President's Day", which is really just a birthday party for our two most famous presidents—George Washington and Abraham Lincoln. I don't expect that birthdays in America are much different than birthdays anywhere else around the world, although you may find a few strange differences. Don't be surprised if you receive one birthday spanking for each year you have been alive or making a wish that may come true upon blowing out all of your birthday candles. Birthdays are always fun so why not celebrate one American style at least once in your life.

DID YOU KNOW?

Did you know that a central and South American tradition of piñatas on your birthday is very popular with children in the United States? A piñata is an animal made out of paper mache that is filled with candy. Children are blindfolded, spun in circles and then they try to break open the piñata using a large stick. When finally opened, all the children scramble to pick up as much candy as they can.

AMERICAN SLANG

I was on "cloud nine" all day on my birthday. (I was feeling fantastic!)

STATE of the UNION

Mississippi State Capital - Jackson

EXCHANGE STUDENT

91 - BIRTHDAYS

Consider yourself lucky if you are able to celebrate your birthday in America, because it may be your only chance. Big cakes with birthday wishes and a lot of frosting are typical and they are usually decorated with your favorite hobby or something crazy. You can either make these cakes or buy them at a grocery store where you have your choice of frosting flavors and colors. Americans also decorate their houses with balloons and streamers for birthday parties and for my birthday my host family decorated with red, white and blue to represent the American Flag. A typical teenage American birthday party consists of a dinner with your favorite food (like pizza or hamburgers) and birthday cake with a candle representing every year of your life. Sleepovers with your best friends are common and most kids stay up most of the night watching movies, playing video games or just talking until you all fall fast asleep. Of course your birthday is not official till your friends and family sing "Happy Birthday to you..." which I found out was written by two American Girls in 1893 and is now universally used.

FACTS...

- Special birthdays are 16, 18, 21, 30, 40, 50, etc.
- Sweet 16 is a young girl's favorite birthday and is typically celebrated with a "slumber" party.
- 18 years old is the official age of adulthood and is usually celebrated during the last year of high school.
- 21 is the legal age for drinking alcohol and is often celebrated just as you might think.

HOST PARENT

92 - EXCHANGE PARTIES

Many exchange parties include the host family and since we were new at hosting, these were great opportunities for us to meet other exchange students and to learn about their lives and cultures. Several parties included international themes in which students were able to pass a dish of food from their home country. It is also important to meet host parents of other exchange students since you may be spending a significant amount of time with one or two of them. Our exchange student and her exchange friends had many parties at various host homes where they celebrated holidays, birthdays or just had fun watching movies and being friends. Often times exchange parties (with or without the host families) included field trips to such places as cider mills, amusement parks and haunted houses. These parties are fun for both the exchange students and host families and are an important part of the exchange organization.

DID YOU KNOW?

Your local exchange group and your high school will probably have several parties throughout the year. Make sure you attend these parties to build friendships all over the world.

AMERICAN SLANG

We had a huge "bash" with all the exchange students at my school.
(Doesn't everybody know that a bash is a large party?)

STATE of the UNION

Montana Nickname - Treasure State

EXCHANGE STUDENT

92 - EXCHANGE PARTIES

When you begin school you will quickly learn that there are two groups—one large group of American students and one very small group of foreign students. You and your fellow exchange students are in the same situation regardless of your country of origin and, therefore, you immediately have something in common. Fortunately, your new school and your exchange organization will have many social events and your fellow exchange students may become your first and your best friends. Although your exchange organization may discourage you from hanging around other exchange students too much (since you are trying to get immersed into American culture), it is helpful and fun as long as you make it only "part" of your life in America. You may find that your exchange organization is not the only one represented at your school. This is even better since it may have just doubled your chances of parties, field trips and other great social events.

IDEAS...

- International Food Parties
- Pool Parties
- Birthday Parties
- Holiday Parties
- Video Game and Board Game Parties
- Picnics
- Activities from your Home Country

HOST PARENT

93 - MUSEUMS

America may not be very old, but that does not mean it is short on museums (relative to many European and Asian countries). The United States has museums everywhere and for almost every subject. Some of the best museums are in Chicago, New York and Los Angeles. Without question, the very best are in Washington, D.C. Every type of museum can be found in America's Capital City and almost all of them are free. You could spend an entire year in Washington, D.C. and never see all the exhibits. Don't worry if you are not near these locations, there are plenty of museums, aquariums, gardens, zoos and art galleries in every big city and many suburbs. Alright, how about some of my favorites: Air & Space Museum in Washington, D.C., Field Museum of Natural History in Chicago, Greenfield Village in Detroit, Metropolitan Museum of Art in New York City, Polynesian Cultural Center in Hawaii, the San Diego Zoo and Aquariums in Atlanta, Tampa Bay and Monterey. If you get the opportunity to visit any museum, make sure you take it. You won't regret it.

DID YOU KNOW?

The Smithsonian Institution is a complex of 19 museums, containing 137 million artifacts and specimens with approximately 25 million visitors each year. (54) All 19 museums are FREE.

AMERICAN SLANG

Museums are just not my "cup of tea". (This is how American's say that it is something they don't like to do.)

EXCHANGE STUDENT

93 - MUSEUMS

History is not my favorite subject, but when it involves a trip to a museum, then history is not so painful. My host family took me to Washington, D.C. where I was able to check out almost any type of American and World history. In Washington, D.C., I was able to view the American Declaration of Independence in one place while checking out a replica of the Wright Brothers very first airplane in another. At Cape Canaveral (also known as Cape Kennedy) in Florida, I toured the Space Shuttle Facilities and actually walked through replicas of the International Space Station. In Chicago, I came face to face with "Sue" which is the world's largest preserved skeleton of a Tyrannosaurs Rex. But by far, my favorite museum may not be considered a museum at all—Madam Tussaud's Wax Museum, where I was photographed with many celebrities including Tom Cruise, Madonna and even President Obama. Maybe history isn't so bad after all.

TIPS...
Check the museums web site before you go for:

- Discount Coupons
- Museum Hours
- Information on current or special exhibits.

Wear comfortable shoes for spending the day on your feet. Talk to employees and volunteers who will often have great suggestions on things you don't want to miss.

STATE of the UNION
North Dakota State Capital - Bismarck

HOST PARENT

94 - HALLMARK HOLIDAYS

Hallmark is a privately owned company that primarily sells greetings cards for special occasions (like birthdays and anniversaries) and holidays (like Christmas and Easter). The term "Hallmark Holiday" is a term that most Americans associate with "unofficial" (non-government) holidays. Whether these holidays were invented in the back room of the Hallmark company or if they are just highly marketed special days, most Americans celebrate all of them. What is the typical gift to give on a Hallmark Holiday? Well, a greeting card of course, but you can always send special gifts that can be found at Hallmark stores all across the United States. There is one Hallmark Holiday that I enjoy—Father's Day. That's right, a day just for me and since I had an exchange daughter, then that was one more person in the family who treated me "special" for a day. Most Hallmark Holidays are fun and why not have another reason to have a party?

DID YOU KNOW?

Hallmark was founded in 1910 and has been making greeting cards ever since. According to Hallmark, Americans send approximately 141 million Mother's Day cards and 93 million Father's Day cards every year. In the new digital age, Hallmark now offers e-cards to send to your best friends. (55)

AMERICAN SLANG

I think only "airheads" forget Sweetest Day. (Airheads are said to be stupid or shallow people.)

STATE of the UNION

Tennessee Nickname - Volunteer State

EXCHANGE STUDENT

94 - HALLMARK HOLIDAYS

Americans like holidays, but come to think of it, who doesn't like holidays? What might be a little different is the amount of cards that Americans give for these holidays or for just any special time in their lives. They like sending funny, colorful, weird, ironic, sensitive and heartfelt cards every chance they can. There is some debate as to whether the Hallmark company made up the holidays to sell cards or if they just found a way to help people send greetings on holidays that already existed. Personally, I think most of the events already existed in the American culture and Hallmark found a way to get in on the celebrations. No doubt there are some days that might have been made up, but are fun to celebrate anyway. I particularly like Grandparents day and while you are in America, it is a great opportunity for you to send a greeting card to your grandparents at home, whom I am sure will be missing you very much. Not a Hallmark holiday, but a new holiday for me, was St. Patrick's Day, which is a huge celebration in America. This is a holiday celebrated on March 17 to honor Saint Patrick who came to Ireland in 432 to spread Christianity. This is a fun holiday because lots of people are wearing green clothes. If you don't wear green, prepare to be pinched! (look it up)

FACTS...

- Valentine's Day and Sweetest Day are celebrated by giving your sweetheart cards, flowers and/or candy.
- Mother's Day and Father's Day are celebrated by all Americans, usually by a special dinner and a day of relaxation.
- Halloween and St. Patrick's Day are very popular days.

HOST PARENT

95 - SOCIAL NETWORKS

It seems that Facebook and Myspace are taking over the Internet communication world. These and other Internet communication tools have made the life of an exchange student and host family so much easier. Meeting your host family before the exchange is nice, but without a doubt, the best thing about social networking is the ability to stay in contact with your host family well after the exchange year is over, and hopefully, for many years to come. Before the Internet, there was truly finality to your exchange year and your host family became nothing more than a distant memory with an occasional letter or postcard. In today's world, technology has made our world smaller and closer than ever. You can talk to your host family every day by e-mail, Internet chat or video conference calling. Recently, I video phoned my German exchange daughter on Skype, chatted with a past Ukrainian exchange student on Facebook and sent an e-mail to a new student arriving soon from Austria. Let's hope all of this world-wide communication will also bring world-wide peace (or at least a lot of new friends).

DID YOU KNOW?

Did you know that Facebook has over 500 million active users and that about 70% of these users are from outside of the United States with over 70 translations available? The average Facebook user has 130 friends and over 2 billion photographs are uploaded each month. (43)

AMERICAN SLANG

I love chatting with my friends on Facebook, but you do have to be careful of "creepy" people. (Creepy people are strange, weird and often bad people.)

EXCHANGE STUDENT

95 - SOCIAL NETWORKS

There are all kinds of computer based social networks now, but the most popular during my stay was Facebook. Before my exchange year began I had rarely heard of Facebook and now that I am home (in Germany), I use it almost every day. This and other social networks are a great way to see what is going on in my American hometown. I love looking at pictures of all my American friends and family and keeping in touch with what is happening in their daily lives. As you might have guessed, they all love staying in touch we me, following my German life and meeting (through chats and Internet phone calls) my family and friends. You can look at photos, make comments about photos or activities, meet new friends, play games, join social network groups or even chat with exchange friends in other parts of the world. In a way, the Internet and the digital social networks that are now available have made it almost seem like I never left America. In today's world you really can keep both lives. Your family and friends in your home country and your family and friends in your exchange country are just a fingertip away. Please join our group on Facebook called "100 THINGS TO KNOW BEFORE YOU GO".

TIPS...

- Use Skype, FaceTime, iChat or ooVoo to video conference with your host family, your family back home or all of your new international friends.
- Use Facebook or Myspace to upload photos and video to share with friends and family all over the world.
- Use Twitter to follow your favorite people, groups or activities no matter where you are or where they are.

STATE of the UNION

Massachusetts State Capital - Boston

HOST PARENT

96 - BASEBALL

In America they call baseball players "the boys of summer". You will miss most of the baseball season, but you will be here for the most exciting time of the baseball year—the playoffs as they are called. October is when the best professional teams of the year play each other to ultimately make it into the "World Series". If you are asking why they call it the "World Series" when only American (and one Canadian) teams play, I can only say "I have no idea". Maybe because the modern game was invented here and because it is more popular here than anywhere else in the world. You may have never watched this sport, and even more likely, you may have never played this sport. If you get the opportunity, give it a try, because I think it is much more fun to play than it is to watch (see my exchange daughter's story for more information on that subject). If you have got the talent you can even try out for your American high school baseball or softball (girls) team.

DID YOU KNOW?

Did you know Abler Doubleday is said to have fired the first shot of the American Civil War at Fort Sumter in South Carolina, and he also is said to have invented the modern game of baseball. Historians disagree and say this baseball claim is only a myth, but many people believe the story and the baseball "Hall of Fame" is located in his hometown of Cooperstown, New York.

AMERICAN SLANG

My host daughter is really talking "smack" in this story.

(Smack is talking bad about something or "trash-talking".)

EXCHANGE STUDENT

96 - BASEBALL

Alright, by now you have read my host dad's opinion on the game of soccer and therefore it is now my turn. Yes, I agree that you should go see a baseball game. Make sure you go to just one game, unless you are tired and need to catch up on your sleep. This game can go so slow that you begin to daydream and your back starts to hurt from sitting so long in an uncomfortable chair. Americans complain about low scoring soccer games, but baseball is not much better. There are times that nobody is doing anything! Alright, I'll stop and tell you about the positive things at a baseball game. The hotdogs. Yes, the hotdogs are fantastic, and so is the cotton candy, pretzels, pizza, and peanuts. If you like junk food while watching a miserably slow sport, then this is the place for you. The next best things are baseball caps. Sure you can buy a baseball cap just about anywhere. Americans wear them all the time and everywhere. So even if you don't like the sport at least you will be able to buy a trendy new hat to take home.

FACTS...

Here are a few facts, but this is a complicated game and you will definitely need to go to a game with your friends:

- Baseball is played on an "infield" called the "diamond" and an "outfield".
- Baseball has 9 innings and each inning provides both teams a chance to score runs before they get 3 outs.
- Each team has 9 players including a pitcher and a catcher.
- Three "strikes" and the batter is out (strike out), but 4 "balls" and the batter gets a free base.

STATE of the UNION

New Jersey Nickname - Garden State

HOST PARENT

97 - OUTLET MALLS

Outlet stores began as a way for manufacturers to sell directly to their customers. In the early days, it was often a store attached directly to the manufacturer's location, but today you will find entire malls comprised of nothing but these stores. These malls are not everywhere, but you will find several in most states in America. You can find some great savings at these stores, because they eliminate the price mark-up necessary for retailers to make money. You will find even better savings on products that the manufacturer has discontinued and the most savings on items that are considered damaged in some way. If you love shopping, but you really hate to work so hard at finding deals at the regular mall, then the outlet malls are for you. These stores may just be the right place to pick up gifts for family and friends at home.

DID YOU KNOW?

The term "shopping mall" generally refers to enclosed structures while the term "shopping center" typically refers to an open air (outside) retail structure. In America, most people call all retail structures malls and almost all outlet malls are open air.

AMERICAN SLANG

I found a really cool "hoodie" at the outlet mall. (A hoodie is nothing more than a sweat shirt with a hood.)

EXCHANGE STUDENT

97 - OUTLET MALLS

My real dad and my host dad have at least one thing in common. They both have a dislike for malls but that is probably true of most dads. Anyway, that is their problem because my moms and sisters (real and exchange) love malls and so do I. Malls in America are like everything else here, they are mostly huge and some of them have hundreds of stores. Stores found in outlet malls are usually brand names that do not have stores in a regular mall—like Nike sportswear or Waterford china. You will find great deals since many outlet stores are selling discontinued products or items that did not sell very well in stores in the regular malls. If you find that you forgot to pack something from home and you are looking for a great deal, then try and find an outlet mall near your American home.

TIPS...

- Do some online research because most outlet malls provide Internet coupons.
- They generally open earlier and stay open later than regular shopping malls.
- Bring appropriate clothing since you will spend a fair amount of time walking outside.

STATE of the UNION

Wyoming State Capital - Cheyenne

HOST PARENT

98 - SPRING BREAK

Spring break in America is as iconic as baseball and apple pie. Every school and every college in America has a spring break, which is better defined as a "spring vacation". If travelling is involved, usually college students go on spring break with their friends, while most high school students take a vacation with their family. It is very difficult to go on spring break in high school without your family because of the long distances needed to travel and because most hotels and car rental companies will not provide these services to kids under 18 (sometimes under 21). One thing is true, no matter where you go and who you go with, you are ready to take a break from the long winter and it is a great kickoff for the coming spring and summer months. As an exchange student it may always feel like you are on spring break, but now you can take a break from your break. Wow, that sounds like fun, maybe I should become an exchange student.

DID YOU KNOW?

Spring breaks in America are often the week before or after Easter Sunday. Some schools actually have a long weekend for Easter (no school on Friday or Monday) while they still have another week off for spring break. Spring break is almost always in March or April and some students even get a week at Easter and another week. How lucky will you be?

AMERICAN SLANG

The location of our spring break trip is still "up in the air".
(This mean you are unsure.)

STATE of the UNION

Pennsylvania Nickname - Keystone State

EXCHANGE STUDENT

98 - SPRING BREAK

Is there any time of the year as fun as Christmas? If you live in America, I would say yes, spring break in America is awesome! Whether you are in kindergarten, high school or college, everybody gets a week off some time in March or April. Which week you get off depends on what school you attend. One school may have their week off as much as a month before or after another school. Most college age kids may go to a favorite beach spot with other college kids while most high school students and younger go on vacations with their families. My host family was very adventurous and I was lucky enough to take a fantastic trip to the western United States. We visited Las Vegas with its huge casinos and Sedona with its beautiful red rock scenery. We watched some filming of the Miss America Contest, took a ride on a huge roller coaster through the "New York New York Casino" and a jeep ride through the scenic Sedona Mountains. If that's not enough, we even visited one of the seven natural wonders of the world, the Grand Canyon. I was overwhelmed by all the beautiful scenery we saw on our spring break, whether it was the magnificent lights on a hotel or the unbelievable view at the Grand Canyon. Spring breaks should be required for everybody on planet Earth.

FACTS...

There are many fun locations for spring break, but these are some of the favorites depending on where you live in America:

- Mexico, Florida Texas or California (for sun and beaches and amusement parks)
- Colorado, Utah & Canada (for skiing and snow fun)

HOST PARENT

99 - MEMORIAL DAY

Memorial Day in America serves two purposes. First, it is an official holiday created to commemorate U.S. men and women who died while in the military service. Second, because of the date (last Monday in May), it is unofficially the beginning of the summer season. Most communities celebrate Memorial Day with a parade followed by a ceremony honoring those from their city that have died in service of the country. No matter where you are living in America, it is usually a beautiful time of the year with flowers in bloom and warm weather creeping its way into your life. Everybody in America has Monday off and the three-day weekend is both somber in reflection and festive in celebration. When I was a kid my high school band marched in this parade every year and now my kids march with their band. Our exchange student participated as well and we had a great weekend of sun, fun and food with friends and family. When you reach Memorial Day you are near the end of the school year and your exchange year. You are also close to great summer fun and soon will be reuniting with your real family.

DID YOU KNOW?

Memorial Day was established after the American Civil war to honor those Union soldiers who had died while in service to the country (North). This holiday used to be called "Decoration Day".

AMERICAN SLANG

I tripped and fell down in the Memorial Day parade and now my friends have been calling me a "klutz". (This is a clumsy person.)

EXCHANGE STUDENT

99 - MEMORIAL DAY

Memorial Day and Labor Day are like bookends holding up your summer vacation. For most American kids Memorial Day is their favorite holiday of the two because it kicks off their summer vacation. It is not as happy for an exchange student because it is a sign that your exchange year is almost over. Many American families take a three-day vacation by camping or traveling to a fun place a short distance away from their home. If you do not go on a holiday with your host family, then make sure you use this time wisely and spend time with your friends. Take it from somebody who has been through it already and enjoy the last few weeks of your exchange year because the time from Memorial Day until the time you leave will go by as fast as a jet plane. Memorial Day brings spring flowers, warmer temperatures and lots of outdoor fun. Even though school is extremely fun in America, Memorial Day comes at a great time to take a break which is needed as you will soon be busy with end of year activities, parties and the ever dreaded final exams.

FACTS...

Facts about the U.S. National Cemetery: (56)

- The official name is Arlington National Cemetery where more than 300,000 military veterans are buried.
- The 200 acre cemetery is on land once owned by the Robert E. Lee family (famous Confederate Civil War General).
- The "tomb of the unknown" solder is located at Arlington and is guarded by a U.S. Marine soldier 24 hours a day.
- Arlington has an average of 28 funerals per day.

STATE of the UNION

Oregon State Capital - Salem

HOST PARENT

100 - MAKING MEMORIES

Well we've reached the end of our book, but this is just the beginning of your experience. Dominique and I have had a lot of fun writing this book and hopefully you have enjoyed reading about our year as a host family and an exchange student. Of course this was just a peek into our time together and the experiences we shared. You are going to create your own memories and therefore you will be writing your own story. You may not put your story into a book, but there are many other ways for you to remember your time in America. You can write a diary, make a scrapbook, take photographs or make a blog. There are so many things you can do to enjoy your year and even more ways for you to etch it in your memory forever. If you are a student reading this in preparation for your trip to America, I hope it has been enlightening. If you are a past exchange student, I hope this has helped rekindle those memories of your time in America. If you are a family considering hosting a student, I hope this helps make up your mind and serves as a guide for the year to come. Whatever your reasons are for reading this book we are very happy you took time to share our memories.

DID YOU KNOW?

Did you know that Dominique and Scott worked on this book for well over one year and half of the book was written by using e-mail and Skype? A life-long friendship has been made and their families have become close friends. You never know how your exchange year will change your life.

STATE of the UNION

Vermont Nickname - Green Mountain State

EXCHANGE STUDENT

100 - MAKING MEMORIES

Writing this last story in our book makes me a little bit sad, but at the same time I am very happy that we have really accomplished our goal to write our own book. When we first had this idea we were both were very excited about it, but we soon realized that it was not going to be easy. We quickly understood it was going to be a lot more work than we expected, but it turned out to be a lot more fun too. Writing our book became part of our lives for well over a year. This book becomes an extension of my exchange year because it will always keep America and my host family in my mind and near my heart. Fortunately, I can always look back and read my own memories forever. We really hope you had as much fun reading this book as we did writing it and just maybe we will have shown you what a wonderful time you could have in the exchange student world. As I approach my final sentence, I can now say that the work was worth it and I'm so glad my host dad encouraged me to keep writing. Who knows, maybe now that this book officially ends my exchange experience, it may have guided me on a new career path. There was one important thing I learned in America; there is nothing I can't do if I work hard enough and if I believe in myself.

FACTS...

- Dominique Kirste started writing this book at only 16 years old and had only 5 years of English before beginning this book.
- Scott wants to spend part of his retirement volunteering and assisting exchange students.

AMERICAN SLANG

These exchange students are the "cream of the crop". (They are the best.)

Tobogganing with friends

Cycling in county park

Museum trip to Chicago

Works Cited

1. **Radicati Team.** Publications. *The Radicati Group, Inc.* [Online] April 20, 2010. [Cited: February 13, 2011.] www.radicati.com/?p=5282.

2. **Relay Health.** Live Well Library. *Summit Medical Group.* [Online] October 2010. [Cited: February 13, 2011.] www.summitmedicalgroup.com/library/sports_health/jet_lag/.

3. **U.S. National Park Service.** National Park Service. *National Park Service.* [Online] U.S. Department of the Interior. [Cited: February 13, 2011.] www.nps.gov/stli/index.htm.

4. **Houghton Mifflin Company.** *The American Heritage Dictonary of the English Language.* Chicago : Houghton Mifflin Company, 2000.

5. **Bellis, Mary.** About.com.Inventors. *About.com.* [Online] [Cited: February 13, 2011.] www.inventors.about.com/od/pstartinventions/a/stilphotography.htm.

6. **Word-Origins.com.** *Word-Origins.com.* [Online] www.word-origins.com/definition/nickel.html.

7. **Clyde Kluckhohn, A.L. Kroeber, Alfred G. Meyer, Wayne Unterenes.** *Culture: A Critical Review of Concepts and Definitions.* Cambridge : Peabody Museum, 1952.

8. **U.S. National Park Service.** Ellis Island History. *www.ellisisland.org.* [Online] U.S. National Park Service. [Cited: February 19, 2011.] www.ellisisland.org/genealogy/ellis_island_history.asp.

9. **U.S. Census Bureau.** Languange Use. *U.S. Census Bureau.* [Online] U.S. Census Bureau, April 2010. [Cited: Febraury 19, 2011.] www.census.gov/hhes/socdemo/language/.

10. **U.S. Postal Service.** Postage Rates and Historical Statistics. *United States Postal Service (USPS).* [Online] U.S. Postal Service. [Cited: February 19, 2011.] www.usps.com/postalhistory/ratesandhistoricalstatistics.htm.

11. **Immigration Road.com.** Visa Bulletin. *www.immigrationroad.com.* [Online] [Cited: February 2011, 2011.] www.immigrationroad.com/resource/visa—bulletin.php.

12. **Where Spirit Leads, Incorporated.** Scrapbook Trivia. *www.disneyscrapbookshop.com.* [Online] Where Spirit Leads, Incorporated, February 8, 2010. [Cited: February 19, 2011.] www.disneyscrapbookshop.com.

13. **Name Administration Incorporated.** *Obesityinamerica.com.* [Online] Name Administration Incorporated, 2007. [Cited: February 19, 2011.] www.obesityinamerica.com.

14. **Senn, James A.** *Three Hundred and Twenty-Five Prompts for Personal*

Journals. s.l. : Schoolastic Books, 1995. 0590493507.
15. **Miniwatts Marketing Group.** *Internet World Stats.* [Online] Miniwatts Marketing Group, October 2010. [Cited: February 26, 2011.] www.internetworldstats.com/stats.htm.
16. **Leichtman Research Group, Inc.** Press, November 15, 2010. *Leichtman Research Group.* [Online] Leichtman Research Group, Inc., November 2010. [Cited: February 26, 2011.] www.leichtmanresearch.com.
17. **Living Internet.** *Living Internet.* [Online] Living Internet. [Cited: February 26, 2011.] www.livinginternet.com/i/ii_licklider.htm.
18. **Old and Sold.** Stereotyping. *Old and Sold.* [Online] Old and Sold. [Cited: February 26, 2011.] www.oldandsold.com/articles09/stereotype-4.shtml.
19. **Sweet Additions.** Food and Drink. *Sweet Additions.* [Online] Sweet Additions, May 25, 2010. [Cited: February 26, 2011.] www.sweetadditions.net/food-drinks/fast-food-statistics-in-united-states-of-america.
20. **U.S. Department of Transporation, National Highway Traffic Safety Administration.** *Fatality Analysis Reporting System.* [Online] U.S. Department of Transportation. [Cited: February 26, 2011.] www-fars.nhtsa.dot.gov/Main/index.aspx.
21. **International Jelly and Preserve Association.** Jams and Jelly Lore. *Jelly.org.* [Online] International Jelly and Preserve Association. [Cited: February 26, 2011.] www.jelly.org/lore.html.
22. **U.S. Census Bureau.** Population Estimates. *U.S. Census Bureau.* [Online] U.S. Department of Commerce, 2009. [Cited: February 26, 2011.] www.census.gov/popest/national/asrh/natasrh.htm.
23. **Neal, Rome.** *Personality Traits Linked to Birth Order.* [Television, CBS Early Show] New York : CBS News Worldwide Incorporated, CBS Worldwide Incorporated, 2002.
24. **American Kennel Club.** AKC News. *American Kennel Club.* [Online] American Kennel Club, January 27, 2010. [Cited: February 2011, 2011.] www.akc.org/news/index.cfm?article_id=4044.
25. **Emily, Executive Producer, Discovery Company.** Top Dog and Cat Names of 2010. *Pet Finder.* [Online] Discovery Company, December 28, 2010. [Cited: February 26, 2011.] www.petfinder.com/blog/2010/12/28/the-top-dog-and-cat-names-of-2/.
26. **Hartford Seminary.** Faith Communities Today. *Hartford Instutute for Religion Research.* [Online] Hartford Seminary, 2010. [Cited: February 26, 2011.] www.hirr.hartsem.edu.
27. **Jamie Frater.** Fact and Fiction. *Listverse.* [Online] Jamie Frater, October 11, 2009. [Cited: February 26, 2011.] www.listverse.com/2009/10/11/10-more-amazing-facts-about-dreams/.
28. **U.S. Census Bureau.** Population Projections. *U.S. Census Bureau.* [Online] U.S. Department of Commerce, January 2000. [Cited: February 26, 2011.] www.

census.gov/population/www/projections/usinterimproj/.

29. **John T. Woolley and Gerhard Peters (from Presdient Jimmy Carter Proclamation 4580).** The American Presidency Project Online. *The American Presidency Project.* [Online] University of California Santa Barbara. [Cited: February 26, 2011.] www.presidency.ucsb.edu/ws/index.php?pid=31142.

30. **Council on Standars for International Educational Travel.** Home Page, 2010-2011 Reports. *CSIET - Council on Standards for International Educational Travel.* [Online] Council on Standards for International Educational Travel. [Cited: February 26, 2011.] www.csiet.org/publications-resources/documents/CSIETSTATSREPORT2010.pdf.

31. **Centers for Disease Control and Prevention.** Healthy Youth, Health Topics, Infectious Diseases. *CDC - Centers for Disease Control and Prevention.* [Online] Centers for Disease Control and Prevention, August 14, 2009. [Cited: February 26, 2011.] www.cdc.gov/healthyouth/infectious/index.htm.

32. **Department of Health and Human Services.** Common Cold. *National Institute of Allergy and Infectious Diseases.* [Online] Department of Health and Human Services, February 11, 2011. [Cited: February 26, 2011.] www.niaid.nih.gov/topics/commoncold/pages/prevention.aspx.

33. **Encylcopaedia Britannica.** *Merriam-Webster Dictionary.* [Online] Encylclopaedia Britannica. [Cited: February 26, 2011.] www.merriam-webster.com/dictionary/senior.

34. **U.S. Department of Agriculture.** National School Lunch Program. *U.S. Department of Acgriculture, Food and Nutritioin Service.* [Online] U.S. Department of Acgriculture. [Cited: February 26, 2011.] www.fns.usda.gov/cnd/lunch/.

35. **NOAA, Department of Commerce.** National Weather Service, Easter Region Headquarters, Winter Storm Trivia Questions. *Eastern Region Headquarters, National Weather Service.* [Online] National Oceanic and Atmospheric Administration. [Cited: February 26, 2011.] www.erh.noaa.gov/er/lwx/winter/TRIVIA.htm.

36. **Unviersity of Colorado at Boulder.** Education Center, Facts about Snow. *National Snow and Ice Data Center.* [Online] University of Colorado at Boulder. [Cited: February 26, 2011.] www.nsidc.org/snow/facts.html.

37. **Yarbrough, Roy E.** *Mascots - The History of Senior College and University Mascots/Nicknames.* s.l. : Bluff University Communications, 2004. 1891248251.

38. **Apple, Inc.** 2007 Press Releases. *Apple.com.* [Online] Apple, Inc., April 9, 2007. [Cited: February 26, 2011.] www.apple.com/pr/library/2007/04/09ipod.html.

39. **Centers for Disease Control and Prevention.** Morbidity and Mortality Weekly Report. *CDS - Centers for Disease Control and Prevention.* [Online] Departemnt of Health and Human Services, September 27, 2002. [Cited: February 26, 2011.] www.cdc.gov/mmwr/preview/mmwrhtml/mm5138a2.htm.

40. **National Sleep Foundation.** *Adolescent Sleep Needs and Patterns, Research Report and Resource Guide.* Washington D.C. : National Sleep Foundation, 200.

41. **Central Intelligence Agency.** The World Factbook. *Central Intelligence Agency.* [Online] Central Intelligence Agency. [Cited: February 27, 2011.] www.cia.gov/library/publications/the-world-factbook. 1553-8133.
42. **U.S. National Park Service.** Frequently Asked Questions. *National Park Service.* [Online] U.S. Department of Interior, December 2010. [Cited: February 27, 2011.] www.nps.gov/faqs.htm.
43. **Facebook.** Press Room. *Facebook.* [Online] Facebook, 2011. [Cited: February 27, 2011.] www.facebook.com/press/info.php?stastics.
44. **Santino, Jack.** American Folklife Center. *Library of Congress Research Centers.* [Online] Library of Congress, September 1982. [Cited: Febrary 27, 2011.] www.loc.gov/folklife/halloween.htm.
45. **National Retail Federation.** Hallowee Headquarters. *National Retail Federation.* [Online] National Retail Federation, 2010. [Cited: February 27, 2011.] www.nrf.com/modules.php?name=Dashboard&id=54.
46. **U.S. Census Bureau.** Facts for Features. *U.S.Census Bureau.* [Online] August 30, 2007. [Cited: February 27, 2011.] www.census.gov/newsroom/releases/pdf/cb07-ff15.pdf.
47. **U.S. Census Bureau.** Facts for Features. *U.S. Census Bureau.* [Online] October 14, 2010. [Cited: February 27, 2011.] www.census.gov/newsroom/releases/pdf/cb10ff-20_thanksgiving.pdf.
48. **Mall of America.** Overview. *Mall of America.* [Online] [Cited: February 27, 2011.] www.mallofamerica.com/about/moa.
49. **Leocha, Charlie.** Today. *Consumer Traveler.* [Online] Consumer Traveler, May 22, 2010. [Cited: February 27, 2011.] www.consumertraveler.com/today/forbes-americas-top-tourist-attractions/.
50. **The Nielsen Company.** Nielsen Wire. *The Nielsen Company.* [Online] The Nielsen Company, May 20, 2009. [Cited: February 27, 2011.] http://blog.nielsen.com/nielsenwire/nielsen-news/americans-watching-more-tv-than-ever/.
51. **National Association of Theatre Owners.** Statistics, Admissions. *National Association of Theatre Owners.* [Online] National Association of Theatre Owners. [Cited: February 27, 2011.] www.natoonline.org/stasticsadmissions.htm.
52. **National Association of Theatre Owners.** Stastics, Screens. *National Associaton of Theatre Owners.* [Online] National Association of Theatre Owners, December 6, 2009. [Cited: Febrary 27, 2011.] www.natoonline.org/stasticsscreens.htm.
53. **Hardman, Derek.** Concert Tickets Reivew. *Top Ten Reviews.* [Online] Tech Media Netwrok. [Cited: February 27, 2011.] www.online-concert-tickets-review.toptenreviews.com/the-biggest-concerts-in-history.html.
54. **Smithsonian Instution.** Collections. *Smithsonian* . [Online] Smithsonian Institution. [Cited: February 27, 2011.] www.si.edu/collections.
55. **Hallmark Card, Inc.** 100 Years of Hallmark History. *Hallmark.* [Online] Hallmark Card, Inc. [Cited: February 27, 2011.] www.corporate.hallmark.com/

History/Company-History.

56. **Arlington National Cemetery.** Visitor Information. *Arlington National Cemetery.* [Online] U.S. Department of the Army. [Cited: February 27, 2011.] www.arlingtoncemetery.mil/index.htm.